GROWING
Good Food

GROWING
Good Food

A CITIZEN'S GUIDE TO
BACKYARD CARBON FARMING

WRITTEN BY ACADIA TUCKER

ILLUSTRATED BY JOE WIRTHEIM

STONE PIER
P R E S S

Stone Pier Press
San Francisco, California

ISBN: 9780998862330

Library of Congress Control Number: 2019946425
Names: Tucker, Acadia, author. Wirtheim, Joe, illustrator. Ellis, Clare, editor.
 Berry, Mary; Biklé, Anne; Brown, Gabe; LaSalle, Tim; Montgomery, David;
 Weaver, Michael, contributors.
Title: Growing Good Food: A citizen's guide to backyard carbon farming

Printed in the United States of America

First Printing: October 2019

23 22 21 20 19   5 4 3 2 1

Cover design by Joe Wirtheim

Designed by Mayfly Design; set in type by Abrah Griggs

Contents

KEEP IT GOING

Questions

Tools for Backyard Carbon Farmers

NOTES

CHARTS & GUIDES

CONTRIBUTORS

CITIZEN GARDENERS UNITE

My backyard garden looks almost nothing like the two–acre market farm I planted in Washington State eight years ago. I still grow tomatoes. And I can't imagine having a garden without onions, or the beans that I eat off the vine every August, which is peak growing season here in New Hampshire. But I no longer plant my favorite melons, and the long rows of squash and corn that took up so much room on my farm have given way to other plants.

The growing season in chilly New England is much shorter than the one in the Pacific Northwest. This means my garden doesn't have as much time to bask in the sun, and long-season, heat-loving crops like watermelon aren't worth the space they need to thrive. Plus, I decided a few years ago to make room for more perennials, which is why there's a much greater representation of rhubarb, blueberries, herbs, and other deep-rooted plants, including peculiar-looking ones like walking onions.

When I first started farming in Washington, my small team and I grew close to 200 varieties of fruits, herbs, and vegetables. Our focus was on planting organic crops and finding enough customers to buy them. We started with the basics, including corn, peppers, and lettuce —the produce we knew people would keep coming back for.

Our location at the northernmost tip of Washington State meant we had more than 15 hours of sunlight a day at the height of summer. For three years I watched, as the summer sun cooked the soil during long periods of unprecedented drought. When it finally did rain, it was torrential and came all at once. Water pooled on the hard, packed dirt and dried up before it could percolate down to where my plants needed it most. At some point, we started to realize these weather extremes were not just a blip but a pattern.

So we learned to push hardier crops on our customers, like currants, raspberries, and asparagus. We threw open our farmstand each Saturday to talk about these changes, and found ourselves fielding questions about other topics as well. Rather than simply asking, as they once had, how to grow something as *beautiful* as what we were offering, customers wanted help in a more urgent way. They needed our advice on dealing with the arrival of new pests from the south, preventing plants from drowning in mud, and irrigating after intensely hot days had sucked the soil dry.

I was struggling with the same problems myself, and they had produced in me a kind of low-level anxiety that made it hard to sleep at night. I was stressed about the future of the farm, and of agriculture. Still, I wanted to keep growing food. So I decided to return to school for a graduate degree in land and water management with the hope of finding some answers.

Even before I began to formally study agriculture I knew that soil, if treated right, could buffer plants from the effects of the extreme weather caused by our warming world. I'd observed that healthy soil holds more water, resists erosion, and warms more quickly in the spring so plants can get going on growing. Healthy soil will support a vast community of important organisms that can recycle nutrients, ward off pests, and naturally aerate the soil. And the more compost, straw, and other organic matter you add to it, the more carbon dioxide it absorbs.

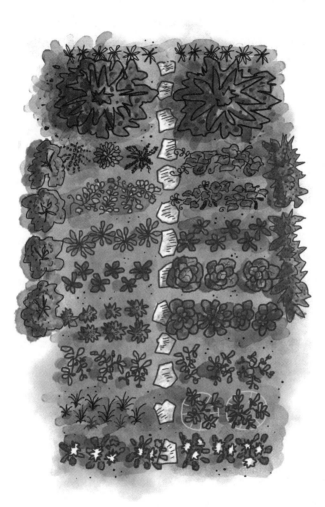

This is a sample Climate Victory Garden. Walking onions, asparagus, berry bushes and other perennials make up most of the garden, but planted among them are lettuce, carrots, and tomatoes. The deep roots of the perennial plants anchor the underground community of soil organisms, even when the annuals planted around them are replaced. A path of flat stones runs through the center of the garden, allowing gardeners to weed and spread compost without stepping on the plant beds and compacting the soil.

For me, learning more about the soil's ability to heal the Earth was life-changing. By the time I finished graduate school, I'd decided to grow food in a way that promotes the build-up of organic matter, which is the essence of regenerative, or carbon, farming. Regenerative practices expand upon the soil's already impressive storage capacity; our natural landscapes absorb 29 percent of all carbon dioxide emissions.

Experts say that regenerative farming, if adopted broadly, could help slow the rate of global warming. With better management, global croplands could store an additional 1.85 gigatons of carbon each year, or as much as the entire transportation sector emits. Researchers at the Rodale Institute calculated that replacing conventional farming practices around the world with regenerative ones would allow us to sequester *100 percent* of annual global carbon emissions.

This means the way we grow food could help save our planet. It is an amazing truth, one that requires major changes in the way farming is practiced. Planting a single crop over vast amounts of acreage, leaving the soil bare for long periods, and relying on frequent plowing accelerates the loss of healthy topsoil, releases buried carbon into the air, and uses up too much water. Poor soil weakens plants and makes them more vulnerable to pests and disease. This necessitates higher levels of chemical fertilizers and pesticides that, in turn, kill the beneficial organisms in the soil that feed plants and help make the soil rich in carbon.

Farmed soils around the world have lost between 50 and 70 percent of their original carbon stocks, according to a recent study from the Carbon Management and Sequestration Center at Ohio State University. Most of that has ended up in the atmosphere. The Environmental Protection Agency (EPA) estimates that farms in this country released nearly 300 million metric tons of carbon dioxide equivalent through poor soil management practices in 2016 alone.

When I returned to the farm with my new degree, I spent my first day walking the grounds of my own small plot, newly attuned to the health of the soil. What I observed was discouraging. So much exhausted dirt! When I tried to water the ground, it was as if the soil was hydrophobic. Where water did sink into the earth, it vanished quickly instead of lingering, robbing my plants of a good drink. In the worst spots, the plants were stunted, clearly starved for water and nutrients.

I began treating the soil by heaping compost under and in between every potato plant, head of lettuce, and row of carrots on my land. Then I layered on a dressing of mulch—grass clippings, straw, and shredded dry leaves—to help prevent the fertilized soil from washing away. I would repeat the entire process in the fall and plant a cover crop of clover, which acts like a living mulch and slows topsoil erosion.

Over that first summer, I added more deep-rooted, low-maintenance perennials to my farm, including radicchio and goji berries. I learned to do without my beloved rototiller, which was a hardship for me—those heavy steel blades truly are the most efficient way to slash through weeds and prep for planting. But tilling and plowing destroy any chance of cultivating healthy soil. For soil-nourishing bacteria, fungi, and other organisms to multiply and thrive, they need an undisturbed place to live.

When I think about how quickly the soil on that little farm responded to my ministrations, I am still stunned. Within a year, the soil had turned a much darker brown. After two years, it was so moist you could squeeze it and it would hold its shape for a long, satisfying moment. Most of my perennials survived the winter, no matter how rainy. Mulching kept weeds to a minimum. And I swear, our tomatoes, beans, and onions were more flavorful. The farm as a whole simply did a better job of taking care of itself.

I left the farm in 2017 because I was homesick for New England's bracingly cold winters and Technicolor falls. I also wanted to see whether I could transfer my regenerative skills to the rocky soil of the Northeast. The kind of soil I associated with picking blueberries as I wandered through the forest until dark.

After I landed a job growing hops for some New England breweries, I immediately planted my own food garden. This time, however, I'm growing food not just for myself or for my business. I'm growing good food—that is, food raised in a way that helps the environment. After seeing the transformation of my own soil, I know how easy it would be to reform our agricultural system, if only there were the political will.

But what if home gardeners made the kind of simple changes I have? What if more of us started carbon farming in our own backyards? What if a community of citizen gardeners joined together to build a giant carbon sink?

It could happen. In fact, it's happened before.

During World War II, Victory Gardens sprouted all over the country. The goal was to support the war effort: more food grown at home for civilians meant more food to send to the troops abroad. It also meant the trucks and trains ordinarily used to transport produce to grocery stores were freed up to move weapons and soldiers. And growing food at home helped families stretch their meager weekly rations.

Posters encouraged citizens to do their part with slogans like "Our food is fighting" and "Food will win the war." People who had never gardened before were energized by the prospect of helping the country, and many Americans gave it a try. Families rallied, clearing and planting vacant city lots, backyards, and schoolyards. People without access to land planted vegetables in pots on stoops and balconies. Others started rooftop and community gardens. Every piece of land was viewed as an opportunity to help win the war. By 1943, the nearly 20 million Victory Gardens across the country were growing 40 percent of the nation's food.

Many decades later, we could use a new Victory Garden movement. We can lobby our leaders to do the right thing by our planet, but we can also take action ourselves. In this country alone, homes, golf courses, and parks grow roughly 40 million acres of turf grass, or about three times the amount of land dedicated to growing corn. More specifically, the average American household maintains a yard a little less than one-fifth of an acre in size, according to 2017 census data. That's a lot of land that could be put to good use as carbon-sucking mini farms.

This book expands on what I started with my first book, *Growing Perennial Foods*. My goal in both has been to simplify regenerative gardening so that anyone can do it. In this book, I address many of the questions I've heard over the last year from readers and audiences. I also invited a few of the folks who have inspired me—David Montgomery and Gabe Brown among them—to share with you the power and promise of backyard carbon farming.

The food I grow in my family's yard is my Climate Victory Garden. It may be small but, thanks to my wedging in as many perennials as possible and feeding it with compost, it is mighty. The following pages describe how easy it would be to park some carbon in your own soil. Let's build a loamy, spongy, dark-brown, microbe-happy foodscape together. It has been done and it can be done, starting with a patch of soil near you.

"Regeneratively managing living soil offers humanity the greatest hope for drawing down our atmospheric carbon levels. We ignore soil carbon capture at our own peril, and harnessing its power can start right in our own backyards."

—Tim LaSalle
Cofounder, Regenerative Agriculture Initiative
California State University

THE CLIMATE CRISIS IN
YOUR OWN BACKYARD

The Earth's climate is changing faster during our lifetimes than it has at any other point in history. This is indisputable thanks to research done by climate scientists who have worked for decades to give us data we can use to both mitigate the damage, and prepare ourselves for what's to come.

Here's what we know: annual average temperatures in the contiguous United States have increased by about 1.8 degrees Fahrenheit since the beginning of the 20th century, and more than half the carbon spewed into the atmosphere by the burning of fossil fuels has been emitted in just the past three decades.

The last few years have seen record-breaking weather extremes around the world; in the US, those have included long, intense heat waves in the South, drought and flooding in the Midwest, and increasingly frequent and severe storms in the North. Climate change will continue to make the flooding, droughts, and other extreme weather even worse, putting an immense strain on crop production and

CHANGES IN THE LENGTH OF THE GROWING SEASON BY REGION

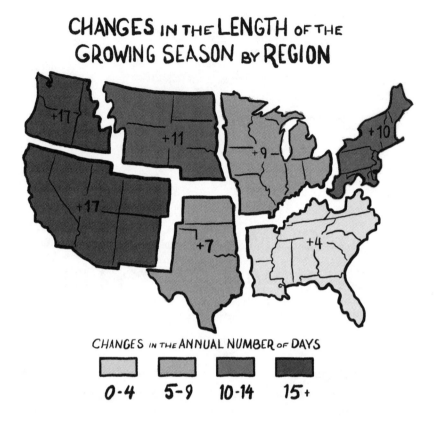

CHANGES IN THE ANNUAL NUMBER OF DAYS

0-4   5-9   10-14   15+

The country's weather is changing at an alarming pace. Since the beginning of the 20th century, the average length of the growing season has increased by two weeks.

resulting in massive global food shortages. A half billion people live in places that are already turning into desert, and the planet is losing soil between 10 and 100 times faster than it is forming.

If we don't take drastic action to slow warming, and *soon*, these extremes will have devastating effects much earlier than researchers were projecting even a few years ago. The Paris Agreement was written in 2015 with the understanding that Antarctic ice sheets were fairly stable, with oceans expected to rise by about three feet by the end of the century. Only two years later, the National Oceanic and Atmospheric Administration (NOAA) suggested an eight-foot rise was possible.

In 2018, the United Nations Intergovernmental Panel on Climate Change (IPCC) reported that there will be severe consequences if global temperatures rise more than 2.7 degrees Fahrenheit above preindustrial levels. If we continue to produce greenhouse gases at our current rate, we will reach that threshold by 2040. Most previous studies had focused on what would happen over a longer timeline, when we reach 3.6 degrees of warming. In sounding the alarm about the catastrophic changes that will happen before that point, the UN report was a crucial wakeup call.

Less than a year later, the IPCC issued another report. This time, it warned that the world's land and water resources are being exploited at "unprecedented rates," which, combined with climate change, puts the entire world at risk of severe food shortages. It cited the dangers associated with the growing global appetite for meat: all those cows, sheep, goats, and other ruminants emit methane, a powerful greenhouse gas. Since 1961, its levels have soared.

Those animals also need pasture on which to graze, and farmers are clearing vast areas of forest every year to meet that demand, releasing the carbon emissions equivalent of driving 600 million cars. The intensifying storms, droughts, and other weather extremes linked to a warming climate are further accelerating the rate of soil loss and land degradation.

Changing the way we grow and manage food could buy us more time. The report's recommendations included increasing the productivity of agricultural land, persuading more people to shift their diets away from meat and dairy and toward plant-based foods, cutting back on food waste, and diversifying crops. The panel also recommended boosting organic carbon content in the soil by adopting the farming practices that regenerative growers are already using.

Working as a farmer has given me an intimate view of how the climate crisis is shaping our world. In Washington, it emerged in the form of lengthening droughts. When I moved to New Hampshire, the challenge became wetter and muddier springs that make it very hard to plant. Still, I was unprepared for the starkness of the findings collected by climate scientists.

Throughout the country, the average length of the growing season has increased by nearly two weeks since the beginning of the 20th century. While a longer summer may seem like a win, rising temperatures also mean that huge swaths of the Southwest are entering a perpetual drought, among other complications. The US Global Change Research Program published its Third National Climate Assessment in 2014. That year was the warmest on record globally. Yet 2015 surpassed it by a wide margin, and 2016 was even worse. Sixteen of the last 17 years have successively broken records for the warmest year ever recorded.

In our warming world, each region faces its own particular set of challenges. Growers have long relied on historic weather trends to make important decisions about what they grow, where, and when. But with weather patterns becoming less predictable, it's a struggle to anticipate the best times to plant and harvest food.

The profiles that follow reflect the forecast for each region in the contiguous US in the Fourth National Climate Assessment, issued in 2018, and what the changes in climate could mean for growers. Each area covers a vast and varied terrain, and there are many exceptions and nuances to these projections that I've left out in the interest of space. But the information here can give you at least a general idea of what to expect in your own backyard.

THE NORTHEAST

Connecticut, Delaware, Maine, Maryland,
Massachusetts, New Hampshire, New Jersey,
New York, Pennsylvania, Rhode Island,
Vermont, West Virginia

Biggest threats to growing food: Extreme precipitation, more pests

What you're used to: We have a saying here: "If you don't like the weather, wait a minute." And it's true that weather can change rapidly in the Northeast from season to season, month to month, minute to minute. It's also true that weather swings between bitter-cold, snowy winters and intensely hot, humid summers.

What's changing: The Northeast's climate swings will become even more extreme in the years to come. Over the last couple of centuries, the average annual temperature in the region has jumped by 2 degrees. By the middle of this century, experts predict, we could see an increase of 3 to 10 degrees above the current average annual temperature, with winters expected to heat up three times faster than summers.

Already, spring is arriving earlier, the summers are hotter, and the winters warmer. The duration of heat waves and droughts is increasing, too. Maryland, Delaware, and southern New Jersey are growing more susceptible to extreme heat waves. Some experts believe that by 2070, we could see heat waves as long as two months.

And there's a twist. Though droughts are becoming more frequent, it's raining about 25 percent more than it did 200 years ago. The reason both can be true is that rain now falls in isolated, extreme storm events rather than over time in a series of rainstorms the soil can more easily absorb. In fact, the Northeast is experiencing up to 70 percent more precipitation during single storm events, raising the risk of flooding. Climate experts predict these downpours will grow even more severe, especially in spring and winter.

What this means for growers: Residents might rejoice over the prospect of milder winters, but plants won't. That's because the Northeast is already experiencing an increasingly irregular cycle of freezing and thawing, and it's hurting them. A warming cycle tricks plants into producing buds and leaves too early in the spring, which means an unexpected deep freeze can kill them. Fluctuating temperatures also cause soil to expand and contract, which can push roots to the surface and expose them to climate extremes. Changes in precipitation mean earlier and wetter springs, which will force farmers to delay planting until their muddy fields can dry out. Summers, meanwhile, will get even hotter and drier.

Warmer winters mean more pests and weeds, since the cold normally helps keep them in check. We'll be forced to do battle with new bugs we've never dealt with before, and those atrocious ticks carrying Lyme and other diseases are likely to widen their range northward. There's also a risk of West Nile virus moving north, which means lots more bug spray for gardeners.

Overall, gardeners in this region will have to confront a whole host of new challenges, ranging from muddy yards and unpredictable winter and spring temperatures to strange new bug invasions.

SOUTHEAST

Alabama, Arkansas, Florida, Georgia,
Kentucky, Louisiana, Mississippi,
North Carolina, South Carolina,
Tennessee, Virginia

Biggest threats to growing food: Heat waves,
flooding, intense hurricanes

What you're used to: This region is big and includes many different landscapes, from the Appalachians to the Everglades, so it's hard to make broad generalizations. But the Southeast as a whole is no stranger to extreme storms, hurricanes, and tornadoes. It gets about 50 inches of rain a year, much of which falls on the Gulf Coast and Atlantic shore.

What's changing: Unlike the rest of the country, which is steadily warming, the Southeast has been cycling between cooler and warmer periods since the 1930s. This high variability in temperature initially made it hard to detect warming trends, but that started changing in the 1970s. Since then, although average annual temperatures have stayed relatively stable, the average summer temperature has increased by two degrees, and the period from 2010 to 2017 was hotter than any previous time period on record.

Climate models suggest that if emissions do not abate, the Southeast could see average temperatures jump four to eight degrees from current levels by 2100. This would mean a considerable increase in heat waves and droughts coupled with less frequent freezing temperatures in the winter. Already, 61 percent of southeastern cities are experiencing worsening heat waves—a greater percentage than in any other region.

Anticipated changes in rainfall are all over the map, but it appears the northeastern parts of the region will see rainier autumns, while the southwestern areas will see less rain during the summers.

Hurricane season is already longer than it used to be, and Category 4 and 5 storms, the most severe, have been increasing in frequency since the 1980s. There's disagreement among climate experts as to whether we can expect even more hurricanes, but one trend is clear: however many we have, they will be stronger and more likely to carry up to 30 percent more precipitation if they make landfall compared to what we've seen so far.

Rising sea levels are also a major concern for the expanse of low-lying land in the Southeast, and not only in coastal areas. Inland flooding will become more common because even slight increases in sea level can overwhelm municipal drainage systems. With nowhere to go, the rain from the increasingly intense hurricanes will result in longer, more widespread flooding.

What it means for growers: The continued rise in summertime temperatures across the Southeast means plants will suffer more heat stress, which in turn means crop yields will fall. And the impact isn't isolated to summer crops; warming winters have a big impact on perennial crops as well. Fruit trees, for example, require fixed amounts of time in freezing temperatures to stay productive. Apple trees bloom only after about 400 "chill hours." And peaches, an important southeastern crop, need a chill period and warm temperatures at specific points in their development. In the future, we can expect the South to be completely free of frost, severely threatening fruit production.

The sea-level rise and more intense hurricane season will mean formerly productive farmland and gardens will be rendered useless as saltwater creeps higher, damaging crops and cropland permanently. The increase in extreme storms that bring high winds, torrential rains, and flooding also makes crop damage more likely because gale-force winds can rip plants out of the ground and compact soil, making it harder for roots to push through the ground and for soil organisms to breathe.

MIDWEST

Illinois, Indiana, Iowa, Michigan,
Minnesota, Missouri, Ohio, Wisconsin

Biggest threats to growing food:
Soil erosion, rapid warming, floods

What you're used to: It helps to come from hardy stock if you live in the Midwest. Arctic air and massive snowstorms are regular features of winter, and summers bring stifling heat and humidity. Temperatures can swing by more than 100 degrees between seasons, and rain or snow falls most weeks.

What's changing: Temperatures in the Midwest are rising rapidly. Over the last 100 years, the average annual temperature has increased by more than 1.5 degrees. More alarming is how quickly the air has warmed in recent years. Between 1980 and 2010, the average annual temperature warmed three times faster than in previous decades, with the biggest increases recorded in nighttime and winter temperatures.

Overall temperatures in the Midwest are on track to rise another 5 to 7 degrees by the middle of the century. Scientists expect the number of superhot days (95 degrees or more) in a row could reach almost a month by 2070. They predict the northern stretches of the region will warm faster, but the southern stretches could experience longer and more frequent heat waves.

The biggest concern for midwesterners may well be the rise in extreme storms. Since the 1960s, their frequency has jumped by 30 to 40 percent. And they're wetter, too: 40 percent more water is dumped, on average, with each storm.

What it means for growers: The continued rise in summertime temperatures will hit growers hard. There's a good chance that by midcentury, it could be too hot for too long for crops like corn to grow well. Since a warmer atmosphere holds more moisture, downpours will become even more intense. Farmers and gardeners living near rivers and streams are particularly vulnerable to the threat of long-lasting floods.

Heavy rains will also accelerate the rate of soil erosion, and growers can expect the increase in springtime rains to delay spring planting dates because the ground will be too wet and muddy for seeds to take hold. Given that two-thirds of the Midwest is farmland, the country will see a significant decline in agricultural productivity overall.

SOUTHERN GREAT PLAINS

Kansas, Oklahoma, Texas

Biggest threats to growing food:
Extreme heat, water stress

What you're used to: The climate in the Southern Great Plains varies from the arid high elevations in the west to the flat, rolling prairies in the east. This region sees some of the most extreme weather patterns in the country, which can include hurricanes, flooding, massive hailstorms, tornadoes, gusting winds, and dangerously long heat waves and droughts. For the citizens of the Southern Great Plains, anything can happen at almost any moment.

What's changing: Over the past century, the average annual temperature in this region rose by 1 to 2 degrees, and it's likely to get worse. By 2050, temperatures will likely jump by another 3 to 5 degrees. One result will be a rise in the number of 100-plus-degree days: extremely hot conditions now last for about a week a year, but scientists expect that to quadruple by 2050. The increased risk of drought will be most pronounced in the southeastern horn of Texas.

Since the beginning of the century, the frequency of extreme storms has increased by about 40 percent. But unlike storms in the rest of the country, their intensity hasn't changed all that much. In an interesting new pattern, it's now more likely that long droughts will follow big flood events. In 2017, Hurricane Harvey hit Texas, bringing close to 50 inches of rain and relentless winds. More than 30,000 people were evacuated from their homes, and 88 people died. Only a few months after this disaster, nearly 40 percent of the state was experiencing drought, up from just 4 percent before the hurricane hit.

Understanding the effects of this new superwet-to-superdry swing is becoming an important focus for climate experts. Some research suggests the region could become drier than it has ever been in the last 1,000 years.

What it means for growers: Gardeners will have to rely on irrigation to help fruits and vegetables weather the long, hot summers. Since water supplies are already at risk due to aquifers being depleted faster than they can refill, it's likely growers will be subject to tougher water restrictions. The hotter temperatures will also worsen pest and weed problems all over the region. Agriculture may have to relocate to cooler northern zones as summer heat stress and the lack of water threaten crop yields. At its worst, the intense heat could prevent crops from growing at all.

NORTHERN GREAT PLAINS

Montana, Nebraska, North Dakota,
South Dakota, Wyoming

Biggest threats to growing food:
Variable water supply, severe drought

What you're used to: In the Northern Great Plains, rolling prairie gives way to forest and jagged mountain ranges. The eastern part of the region typically gets enough rain to support agriculture, but it's vulnerable to regular flooding. The central portion, home to many ranching operations, is fairly arid; only a fraction of its precipitation reaches the Missouri River as runoff due to high temperatures and rates of evaporation. The mountainous western area, which includes central and western Wyoming and Montana, is mostly wilderness and relies partly on snowpack for its water supply.

What's changing: In the first 20 years of this century, the average temperature here jumped by two degrees. One big driver is North Dakota, where temperatures are rising faster than in any other state.

It's no surprise the region is expected to become even warmer, and that will mean smaller snowpacks as more water falls as rain than as snow. Since water won't be stored in frozen form as long, rivers and reservoir levels will be much lower during late summer and early fall.

While experts don't anticipate a significant change in the amount of precipitation overall, the hotter climate means more water will be lost through evaporation. One outcome of all these changes is a higher likelihood of severe flooding and drought.

What it means for growers: If you live in the eastern part of the region, you'll see wetter winters and springs, which could boost plant growth. But that change also means a shorter growing season because of having to wait until the muddy ground dries to plant seeds.

In the western areas, drought and floods will be an issue for growers as rainfall becomes increasingly variable. Lower snowpack levels and earlier peak snowmelt runoff will produce wetter springs but leave less water for growers in the summer.

Throughout the entire region, residents can expect the total number of winter storms to decline, but they'll be more intense. As snow and rain falls in more concentrated bursts, the rate of soil erosion will accelerate, and soil will suffer. The regional snowpack is also expected to shrink as more winter storms bring rain instead of snow at higher elevations.

NORTHWEST

Idaho, Oregon, Washington

Biggest threats to growing food:
Changes in water runoff levels, wildfires

What you're used to: The Northwest is famous for its jagged coastline and rugged north-to-south mountain ranges. The area west of the mountains tends to be fairly mild, with wet winters and dry summers. To the east, the weather is more variable, with brutally cold winters and stiflingly hot and dry summers. Outdoor recreation is a hallmark of this region, where forest covers almost half the land base.

What's changing: The average annual temperature in this part of the world rose by over one degree between 2000 and 2020. Although the amount of precipitation overall increased within the same period, rising temperatures meant that more of it fell as rain than snow. One result is that the average spring snowpack in the Cascade Range has fallen by 20 percent, and spring snowmelt is taking place a month earlier in some areas. By the middle of the century, snowmelt will likely be happening another three to four weeks earlier.

The end of the century could see temperatures rise another 3 to 10 degrees if we fail to lower the rate of greenhouse gas emissions. In that time frame, experts predict summer rainfall overall will decline by up to 30 percent, with more heavy downpours and snowmelt taking place at lower elevations. The swing between too much and too little water will raise the risk of landslides and floods as well as drought, heat waves, and wildfires.

In 2015, the low snowpack combined with spring and summer droughts led to the region's most severe wildfire season in recorded history, with more than 1.6 million acres burned. The risk of massive wildfires will only become greater as warming and droughts intensify.

What it means for growers: Warmer winters, smaller snowpacks, and earlier melting times will lead to a higher likelihood of drought, water scarcity, and a longer, more devastating fire season, particularly in the eastern reaches. Increasing temperatures have already invited many new pests into the area, like the mountain pine beetle, which has decimated forests. Over the next 15 years, local experts believe more than three million acres, or one-third, of eastern Washington's forests will be riddled with devastating bugs. The resulting dead and dying trees will become tinder for the next fire season.

SOUTHWEST

*Arizona, California, Colorado,
Nevada, New Mexico, Utah*

Biggest threats to growing food:
Wildfires, water scarcity

What you're used to: The Southwest, a mixture of steep peaks, fertile river valleys, and inland deserts, is the country's hottest and driest region. Summertime temperatures can be blazing, reaching as high as 125 degrees in some places. The entire region shares the problems of low rainfall and relatively scarce water supplies. In California, agriculture accounts for about 62 percent of the state's water use.

What's changing: Temperatures rose in the Southwest by nearly two degrees from 2000 to 2020, and the first decade of the century was the hottest ever recorded. By the second half of the century, southwesterners can expect average annual temperatures to rise by at least another three to five degrees, even if we significantly reduce greenhouse gas emissions. If we carry on as usual, without making any effort to limit global warming, temperatures could rise by more than nine degrees. In either scenario, summer heat waves will grow even longer and more relentless.

It's unclear how much rain will fall in the coming years, but it almost certainly will not be enough to stave off frequent periods of drought. The number of extreme storms is on the rise, particularly in California's coastal mountains and the Sierra Nevada, which will increase the risk of mudslides.

What it means for growers: Hotter summers during the growing season will force the area to balance water demands with low water supplies. Southwesterners will almost certainly face water shortages, making it difficult to grow food in California's Central Valley, one of the nation's most important food-producing regions. Wildfires, already moving much faster and burning hotter than ever, are a major concern. Since the 1970s, the total area burned by wildfires has grown by 650 percent.

Most of us don't think much about the soil, let alone its health. But we should.

Since the American Revolution, our nation's agricultural soils have lost half their organic matter. The global situation is comparable. But we can flip this problem on its head and bring soils back to life all around the world. It is one of humanity's best ways to make rapid progress on the daunting challenges of feeding everybody, weathering climate change, and conserving biodiversity.

Regenerative farming is attracting a lot of attention as a way to reverse declining soil fertility while also pulling a lot of carbon out of the atmosphere and stashing it back in the ground, among other benefits. Yet restoring soil health is not just for farms. It is something we can do in urban places, too, and gardeners can lead the way in their small corners of the world.

When we bought a century-old house in North Seattle, we saw firsthand how regenerative gardening transformed our yard—and our lives. The house had been built on the far side of the lot, leaving a large side yard. When Anne saw it, she knew it would become our future garden. But we didn't think to look under the hood of the lawn when we hired an inspector to scour the attic, the basement, and the foundation for potential yellow flags.

When the time came to start planting a garden, we realized our mistake. We had dirt, not soil. Not a single worm worked the dry khaki dust of our newly cleared side yard. Our yard lacked half of the recipe for fertile soil. We had the geology—mineral matter. But the biology—soil life—was missing.

So Anne began her organic-matter crusade, collecting it from nearby sources: the neighbors' fallen leaves, cast-off coffee grounds from the local coffeehouse, and composted elephant dung from the city zoo. With all this organic booty, she started making mulches and layering them on top of the new garden beds.

Over the years, we watched nature reassemble an ecosystem as life returned to the yard in stages that mirrored how life evolved on Earth. Microbes arrived first, followed by worms and other creatures crawling around in the soil, the crows that came to eat them, and ultimately a passing bald eagle that snatched a baby crow from the top of our neighbor's tree. Today, a decade and a half later, our soil is a rich, dark brown, awash in microbes and larger forms of soil life.

Digging into the science behind this transformation, we learned the organic matter was feeding the soil, cultivating the beneficial life there, which grew healthier, more productive plants that in turn produced more organic matter. How does this work? It's a partnership. The plants feed the microbes with decaying organic matter. The microbes help the plants get nutrients out of the soil particles, recycle organic matter into forms the plants can take back up, and tee up plant defenses to help ward off pests and pathogens.

How much of a difference can regenerative gardening make? We took our soil from about one percent organic matter to almost 10 percent, parking tons of carbon in the yard. Imagine if gardeners and farmers all around the world did the same thing. It could change the world.

There's nothing magical about building fertile soil. It's all about learning to work with instead of against soil life. Healthy fertile soil is the foundation for a productive, rewarding garden, just as it is for a farm. The takeaway? What's good for the earth is good for us too.

—Anne Biklé and David R. Montgomery,
Professor of Earth and Space Sciences at the University of Washington
Authors of The Hidden Half of Nature: The Microbial Roots of Life and
Health and Growing a Revolution: Bringing Our Soil Back to Life

OUR GOOD EARTH

When I lived in California, I heard about a chance to take over an old and derelict plant nursery in northern Washington and turn it into a farm. I signed on, knowing it wouldn't be easy—but it was so much harder than I thought.

When I arrived, the pastures were filled with enormous stalks of thistle and curly dock. The battered greenhouses shook in the wind, and every outbuilding needed repairs. Most alarming was all the construction fill, a mixture of broken rocks once used to level the land that almost completely covered the property. The first time I tried to dig into the rubble-strewn dirt, I thrust a pointed shovel—hard!— into the ground. The shovel head bounced back in my hands, leaving me with a sore wrist and only the faintest of impressions in the dirt. This was maybe not a good place to start a farm.

To get around our crappy dirt problem, as we called it, my two partners and I spent the first winter together building as many cedar raised planting beds as we could, filling them with store-bought organic soil. We thought the beds would give us our best shot at quickly growing food, but hadn't bargained on how many we'd have to build to make it commercially viable to grow food, nor how expensive cedar boards can be. The raised sides increase the soil's sun exposure, which dries it out more quickly and meant the beds had to be irrigated, too.

Hoping to find a good in-ground solution to our fill problem, we turned to a fallow pasture on the perimeter of the farm. It was brimming with dandelions, chicory, and plantain and came with its own set of challenges. The weeds had been left to grow, and they had—so vigorously the spiky-leafed thistles were shoulder high. So we did what most farmers do: we brought in a tractor to break up the soil and till the weeds back into the ground.

Big mistake.

After the tractor passed up and down the field a few times, I noticed a glint of something dark and shiny just below the surface. I yelled at the tractor to stop and knelt to see what it was. Teeny pieces of black plastic, millions of them. I guessed they'd come from a thick sheet of landscape fabric that had once been used to smother weeds and become buried over time. I tried not to cry.

I think of this story often when talking with people about regenerative gardening. Building good soil is a critical part of becoming a backyard carbon farmer because all that organic matter helps heal the planet. But it's also a really handy skill to have in case of emergencies, like the one we were having.

For us, repairing that field so it could eventually grow food meant laying down sheets and sheets of cardboard on the plastic-ruined dirt and alternating layers of compost, grass clippings, seaweed, and leaves on top of it. This process, called sheet mulching, produces a big pile of organic matter that eventually breaks down, leaving behind a rich and fertile garden bed—no digging required.

To sheet mulch such a large area, we needed help from the community. We asked local landscapers to drop off their grass clippings. We offered to rake people's yards in exchange for keeping the leaves. We dumpster dived for cardboard behind the grocery store. We called local utility companies and asked them to drop off wood chips left over from fallen and pruned trees. And we collected garden clippings from all around town. Eventually, we amassed enough debris to sheet mulch half the pasture.

By the time we were done, the overgrown pasture had been transformed into a giant compost heap that would decompose over time into beautiful soil. We layered extra compost into evenly spaced rows running the length of the field, two feet apart, that would eventually become the space for planting. After covering these rows with old hay, we waited.

The following spring, the field was weed-free and ready for plants. I raked away the hay to find a layer of gorgeous black soil. The beds were still too shallow for root vegetables but they were just fine for squash, kale, and bush beans. Pretty soon, you couldn't see the ground for the blanket of green leaves. When we harvested that summer, we had more squash than we could sell. I ate so much of it that, to this day, I have a hard time eating the stuff.

HOW SOIL AND PLANTS DRAW DOWN CO_2

Around half of the carbon released into the atmosphere every year is absorbed by oceans, plants, and soil. Soil does most of the heavy lifting, storing four times more carbon than plants. We interrupt this cycle by plowing it, stripping it of forests, spreading chemicals on it, and leaving it bare, and this has terrible consequences. When soil degrades, the molecules that bind carbon break down, releasing it back into the air. Instead of absorbing carbon, depleted soil further contributes to global warming.

Regenerative practices grow food in a way that returns atmospheric carbon back to the soil, a process called sequestration. And it all starts with plants.

Many climate activists promote expensive technologies that pull carbon out of the air and inject it into deep pockets underground. Plants already do this for free through photosynthesis, the process by which light energy is turned into plant food. Every morning, the sun stimulates plants to suck down carbon dioxide. The carbon is

SOIL CARBON CYCLE

ATMOSPHERIC CARBON IS PULLED OUT OF THE AIR VIA PHOTOSYNTHESIS

CARBON LOSS FROM SOIL RESPIRATION & DECOMPOSITION

FALLEN LEAVES & BRANCHES ADD CARBON

CARBON-RICH SUGARS FLOW THROUGH PLANT ROOTS TO FEED SOIL ORGANISMS

Plants are the ultimate carbon sucking machines. They draw down atmospheric carbon through photosynthesis to produce plant food in the form of carbon-rich sugars. Plants use these sugars to grow. They also attract beneficial soil organisms by releasing some of the sugars through their roots. Those molecules of carbon that were once harmful greenhouse gases become tied up in the bodies of microbes, and stored underground.

OUR GOOD EARTH

shuttled through plant cells, picking up new elements along the way, like hydrogen, oxygen, and more carbon. Eventually, it comes to rest in plant tissue as glucose and starch. This is how a molecule of greenhouse gas is turned into the carbon-rich sugar that plants use to grow.

Over time, the carbon gets worked into the soil by bugs and soil organisms as leaves fall and branches break off. But decomposing plant debris accounts for only a fraction of the carbon that gets stored underground. Real carbon sequestration happens deeper, at the roots.

Plants release some of the carbon-rich sugars they make through the tips of their roots to attract bacteria, fungi, and other beneficial microbes. In exchange for the free meal, these tiny organisms offer access to nutrients that plants otherwise can't reach, and even help ward off pests and disease. Now those molecules of carbon, originally drawn from the atmosphere, are tied up in the bodies of soil organisms. When they die, that carbon stays deep underground for as long as it's undisturbed.

Regenerative farming mimics what nature does so beautifully. It leaves plants alone and lets the soil be. In a forest that has been growing for hundreds of years, the plants don't need any fertilizer, irrigation, or pesticides to flourish. When left alone, trees grow, shed leaves, and push down roots that support a community of carbon capturing soil organisms. When they die and fall over, trees create piles of organic material that prevent fertile soil from being washed away. The vast roots left in the ground continue to nourish soil organisms for years to come.

Plants raised in favorable conditions like this, with easy access to moisture and nutrients, grow sturdier, more resilient, and better able to suck down carbon dioxide. This positive cycle is how nature works when we don't interfere.

CULTIVATE GOOD SOIL

Bits of plastic and construction fill weren't the only problems at the farm. The native soil left untouched by the plow was dry and lifeless. When I grabbed a fistful, the sandy grains cascaded through my fingers. Nothing about it resembled the dark color or binding structure of my newly sheet-mulched field. I did some research and pulled up an old soil survey map of the area. It turns out the farm sits on what's classified as Everett soil, a mixture of bits of rock dropped by melting glaciers and covered with silty dust and volcanic ash. It was formed eons ago by the tumultuous natural history of the Pacific Northwest. The coarse soil was drought prone, and I had to irrigate the field as soon as the winter rains stopped.

I couldn't change the inert mineral foundation of the native soil, but I could bring it to life. All I'd have to do is add organic matter.

Organic matter is the superstar ingredient in healthy soil. It's the shredded leaves you spread as mulch, the kitchen scraps you add to your compost heap, the old roots left to decompose underground. Basically, it's anything that was once living.

Hungry soil organisms break down these dead leaves, roots, and scraps and convert them into plant nutrients, like phosphorus, nitrogen, and potassium. This process, known as decomposition, produces humus, a dark brown material that is 60 percent carbon. Humus is very stable and, if undisturbed, can remain in the soil for hundreds or even thousands of years.

Soils rich in organic matter soak up water and nutrients because the molecules are charged, sort of like the static cling that makes a sock stick to your shirt when you pull your clothes out of the dryer. This charge holds moisture and nutrients tight so it's less likely they'll evaporate or wash away. Increasing organic matter in your soil by just one percent can increase its water-retaining ability by an extra 20,000 gallons per acre.

Increasing the percentage of organic matter in the soil also feeds mycorrhizal fungi, vast networks of fungi that release glomalin. Glomalin is a sticky, gum-like substance that binds together particles of sand, silt, and clay, creating a soil structure that further helps to lock in moisture and hold on to nutrients.

Remedying the farm's lifeless dirt took effort. I concentrated on building great piles of compost and mulch and then, twice a year, spreading thick layers of it onto my land. In a few short years the organic matter content in the soil jumped by five percent. It was dark, moist, entirely different from the first handful I'd held. The food it produced was more resistant to pests and better able to withstand the swings from dry weather to wet, and back. And our annual yield jumped—by a lot.

TAKE MEASURE OF YOUR SOIL

The first step toward creating good soil is figuring out what you're starting with. If your land already supports healthy plants, it's probably in pretty good shape to begin with. In this instance, your biggest challenge may be weeding. If what you see instead are stunted plants and bare, dry patches of dirt, it might make sense to build your soil from scratch or grow your food in a raised plant bed.

A good way to learn what's going on underground is to get your soil tested. A soil test tells you the nutrient and pH levels in your soil, allows you to fine-tune your fertilizer use, and establishes a baseline reading so you can evaluate your soil health over time. It can also alert you to any unsafe toxins hidden in your soil.

I spoke recently at an event on the importance of testing your soil before planting a food garden. A woman in the audience told us she had ripped out her lawn a few years ago in favor of an edible landscape and couldn't wait to eat right out of her front yard. But when the results of a last-minute soil test arrived, hers tested positive for lead. Lots of lead. Disappointed, she had to rip up her yard all over again. Case made.

See whether your local state university extension office offers soil testing, or order a kit online. Either way, it will come with instructions on how to gather samples. Once you've submitted them, it takes about two weeks to get the results, which can identify any trouble spots. Most soil tests come back with recommendations about how to amend your soil to grow healthier plants. While the results offer advice on how much of a nutrient to add (usually in pounds per acre), they do not tell you what ingredients will do the trick. For more information on organic fertilizers go to page 141, or talk to your local garden center experts for their organic recommendations.

All that said, many regenerative growers, myself included, skip using specific fertilizers in favor of heaping on more compost and mulch. Over time, it's often enough to fix most soil problems.

CLEAR YOUR PLOT

Before creating any new soil, you have to weed your plot. Since backyard carbon farmers can't rely on the soil-demolishing strength of steel-bladed rototillers, use a mower or scythe to bring weeds and grasses down to a manageable stubble. You can then vanquish what remains of the annuals fairly quickly by covering them with a weed barrier, like cardboard.

Perennial weeds are much tougher to destroy. Their robust roots store so much energy that when the green tops are removed, they quickly grow back. Cardboard barriers don't work because perennials just break through them.

This means the cleanest way to rid yourself of these tenacious plants is to dig out the entire root system. I use a trowel or shovel, or drive a potato fork into the center of the weed and move it back and forth until it comes loose. You can also scorch, or solarize, perennials. To do this, sprinkle the ground with water and lay a heavy sheet of plastic on top of it. In four to six weeks, your weeds will be gone— *boom!*—and you're ready to plant. This process can harm the very soil organisms you want to keep around. But it also kills stubborn weeds, weed seeds, and soil pathogens, like fungal wilts. When you remove the plastic, the good bacteria and fungi quickly return to the solarized patches.

Maybe all this sounds like too much work, because it certainly can be. You can opt to simply mow weeds as close to the ground as possible, and just pull or cut back weeds as you see them. The new growth drains the energy reserves stored in the roots and, if you keep cutting them back, even perennial weeds will eventually give up and die.

BUILD YOUR PLANT BED

Building soil from scratch by way of sheet mulching is my go-to method for starting a new garden. It allows you to build good soil while eliminating weeds, all without digging, plus it works well for just about any space. Creating soil does take time, however, and calls for a hefty supply of leaves, grass clippings, cardboard, and other organic material, so it's not for everyone.

A) **Produce soil from the bottom up, or sheet-mulch.** Once you've mowed and cleared your land, it's time to lay down a barrier to discourage weed growth. I like cardboard, preferably the type without a glossy coating. It smothers weeds and eventually decomposes, adding new organic matter to the soil. Thick layers of newspaper or brown paper bags work the same way.

Before laying down your weed barrier, water the soil thoroughly so it stays moist for as long as possible. Overlap the pieces of cardboard or thick paper by at least four inches so new weeds struggle to find a way to the surface.

Now it's time to build your bed. This is when materials you once deemed a nuisance suddenly become valuable. Those leaves you rake in the fall? That old pile of brush in the corner? The stack of newspapers and boxes you forgot to haul to the dump? They all have a new purpose, which is to build living soil.

I start by shoveling a layer of wood chips onto the weed barrier, followed by grass clippings, then dry leaves or straw, and finally composted food scraps. The order doesn't matter as long as you alternate between green materials (like grass and food scraps) and brown materials (like wood chips, dry leaves, and straw). Continue this process until your bed is at least eight inches high.

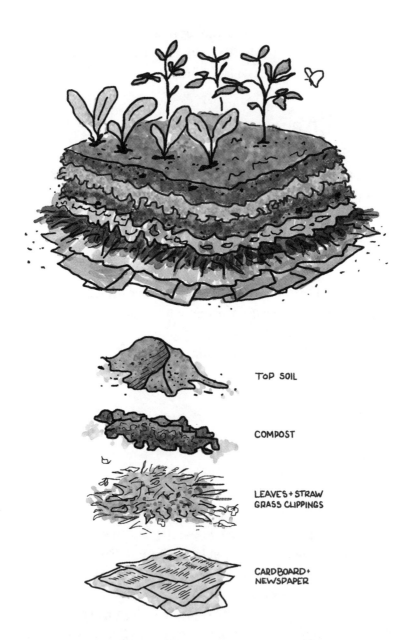

TOP SOIL

COMPOST

LEAVES + STRAW
GRASS CLIPPINGS

CARDBOARD +
NEWSPAPER

Sheet-mulching involves building your garden bed from the bottom up, starting with a layer of moistened cardboard and followed by alternating layers of green and brown materials. Not only will you smother weeds, you'll produce a nutrient-rich bed without doing any digging at all.

You have now created a huge pile of debris, and it isn't pretty. But give it time. One reason gardeners often do their sheet mulching in the fall is to give the organic material time to break down before the planting season begins. If you want to accelerate the decomposition process, include a few extra thick layers of compost in your bedding—and watch your ungainly pile shrink before your eyes.

But you don't have to wait until the pile has shrunk to plant tubers, transplants, or seeds. Pull back the top layers of your pile until you get down to the weed barrier, then use a razor blade to cut an X in the barrier and peel back the corners to make a square hole. Dig your hole, push in a tuber or transplant, then throw in some compost, add water, and cover it all up with dry leaves and straw. If you want to plant a row of seeds, pull back the top layer of mulch and make seed furrows. While your new plants are sprouting, the organic materials will continue to decompose.

B) Just add compost. Maybe all signs point to your soil being fairly healthy. It drains well, supports plant life, and holds its shape pretty well when you squeeze it into a ball. Perhaps you have an existing garden and don't want to start from scratch. Or maybe you don't want to put in the time to sheet mulch, or deal with all that cardboard. If so, you can opt for treating your existing soil with compost.

Once you've cleared your planting area, shovel on two inches or so of compost and mix it into the first few inches of soil. To keep future weeds at bay, add a layer of mulch at least one inch thick on top of the compost. When it's time to plant, simply rake the mulch aside.

Mix compost into your soil every spring. Twice a year, in the spring *and* fall, is even better. Very quickly, the soil should attract enough organisms to support a self-sustaining ecosystem. To maintain it, continue adding about two inches of compost on top of your soil once or twice a year, but going forward there's no need to mix it in. The earthworms, beneficial bacteria, and fungi will do the work for you. Always anchor your compost with a fresh coat of mulch.

C) Haul in new soil. What if fixing your soil with compost isn't an option? Maybe you're dealing with lots of rocks or a cement pad. In these cases, you'll want to create a very thick barrier and then bring in new soil.

A useful shortcut is to build a planting bed out of wood and fill it with organic store-bought soil. But if you decide on an in-ground solution, do your weed-clearing first, then lay down cardboard and heap on at least two inches of mulch. Any mulch will do. (See "Choose your mulch," page 51.) To keep costs down, use leaves, grass, or wood chips—whatever is readily available.

Then bring on the soil. Look for a reputable supplier; some places will resell dirt from construction sites, which is low quality and may contain toxic chemicals. Not good! What you want is an organic soil made for gardening. That way you know it's safe, light, and fast-draining, not compact and heavy like most construction soil.

Bring your store-bought dirt to life by mixing in compost. Aim for a 50/50 blend if possible, but it's also okay to use whatever you've got. Speed up the process, if you like, by adding mycorrhizal fungi, which grow as a vast web of tiny string-like filaments in plant roots and the surrounding soil. Mycorrhizal fungi are the only known fungal system categorized as a living fertilizer because it actually penetrates plant roots to get them the nutrients they need, and helps plants survive disease and drought.

QUESTIONS

How do I know whether I have healthy soil?

Even before I understood the science behind good soil, I knew how to identify it. You do, too. It's the pungent smell of a forest floor after a rainstorm, the look of a wild meadow overrun by brightly colored flowers and tall grasses, the fibrous clod of soil alive with earthworms.

Healthy soil is neither too wet nor too dry. Proper drainage lets water sink into your soil instead of pooling on the surface. Poor drainage is a sign your soil is too compact or heavy with clay, which prevents air from entering and soil organisms from thriving.

While you can't choose your soil, you can drastically improve it with compost. Adding compost to your soil will make it behave more like loam, the perfect growing medium for almost everything. (See "Signs you have good soil," page 44.)

I have contaminated soil. Can I still grow food in it?

Contaminated soil is, unfortunately, a common problem. No matter where you live, there's a chance your soil is polluted.

This country contains more than 400,000 sites the federal government has labeled as contaminated, according to the US Government Accountability Office (GAO). Land located near industrial activity, high-traffic areas, or agricultural zones is often contaminated by substances like pesticides, lead, arsenic, asbestos, and polycyclic aromatic hydrocarbons (toxic chemicals released by burning coal, oil, gas, garbage, or tobacco).

A simple soil test conducted by a local university can tell you whether your soil contains toxins. If you discover it is contaminated, don't lose heart—you may stlll be able to grow food. Only about 15 percent of the total lead concentration in soil is absorbed by plants, according to a 2014 study at Kansas State University. Still, you'll want to clean up this, or any other pollutants, as much as you can.

SIGNS YOU HAVE GOOD SOIL

Figuring out the kind of soil you have is the first step to growing good food. One sign you have healthy soil is if it's supporting healthy plants, but there are other indicators as well, including how well-structured it is and whether or not it contains earthworms. While you can't choose your soil, you can drastically improve it by feeding it regular doses of compost.

Characteristic	Definition	How to know you have it
Well-structured	Pockets of space in between soil particles that make room for water, air, soil organisms, and the healthy growth of plant roots.	Observe how the soil breaks apart when it's neither too wet, nor too dry. You want to see round and crumbly balls that hold up under pressure. If your soil is reduced to flat flakes or single grains of dirt, you have some work to do.

You can also buy a soil penetrometer to measure the force it takes for the probe to enter the soil. Or try this: jam a wire flag, like those used to mark underground sprinkler heads, into the soil. If the wire goes in without bending, the soil is nice and loose. If it starts to bend, the soil is dense and needs to be broken up. |
Drains easily	Easily absorbs and conserves moisture. This is the opposite of compacted dirt, which is packed so hard water pools on top and healthy soil organisms have trouble burrowing into it.	Track how long it takes for rain to soak in. With adequate drainage, any standing water should disappear within 24 hours.
Nutrient rich	Contains the nutrients vital to plant growth, which include potassium, nitrogen, phosphorus, and trace minerals.	A sign your plants are undernourished is if they aren't growing well, rarely bloom, or turn yellow. Another way to find out is by conducting a soil test.
Biologically active	A high level of hardworking soil organisms that work to convert minerals and organic matter into nutrients for plants. They also aerate the soil.	A simple way to test whether your soil is high in biological activity is to see how many earthworms you have. If you see around 10 worms per square foot of soil, it's pretty healthy.

OUR GOOD EARTH

If the soil test shows your soil is highly toxic, hire a professional cleanup company. If you do it yourself, you could ingest contaminants by inhaling dust, plus any soil hauled away from a contaminated area must be disposed of properly. It makes no sense to pollute more land. You'll have to replace all of your dirt with clean soil before growing anything in it.

Even if your soil is only mildly toxic, it's advisable to use proper protection before starting any cleanup project. Wear disposable coveralls, thick gloves, and a sealed respirator mask. You can opt to replace the dirt with fresh soil, which can be a costly production. Or you can create a thick protective barrier. One way to do this is to build a raised planting bed out of wood and fill it with clean soil. Another is to cover the contaminated soil with at least five layers of moistened thick cardboard or a sheet of landscape fabric. Don't leave any cracks or gaps, and top it with a fresh batch of soil or sheet mulch the area.

Pick your plants carefully. Lead and other toxins accumulate more readily in the roots of plants, so stick to growing and harvesting above ground food. In other words, beets, carrots, and potatoes are out. Find out more information from your local university extension center on how best to deal with contaminated soils. The more you know, the safer you'll be.

How do I make compost to use in my garden?

Compost, compost, compost. Sometimes it feels that's all I ever talk about. (My friends would concur.) But there's a reason for it: compost is absolutely critical to Climate Victory gardening. A single application of it was shown to increase the carbon storage capability of California grasslands by 25 to 70 percent compared to neighboring fields without compost, according to the Marin Carbon Project. Even better, soil carbon increases were observed the following year without any additional compost.

By producing your own compost, you can also attack our climate crisis from another angle: reducing food waste. Up to 30 percent of all food produced is lost or wasted. When food ends up in a landfill,

COMPOST MATERIALS

Healthy compost is made from brown and green materials. Aim for a 50/50 mix of the two. If it's not decomposing quickly, add more of the green. If it's smelly and slimy, add more of the brown.

Material	Brown/Green	Notes
Bark mulch	Brown	Bark breaks down more easily than wood chips. It's often available at low cost from a local tree service.
Dried plant waste	Brown	Dead or overwintered plant stalks, crops that have gone to seed, and dried leaves and stems are all a good source of brown compost.
Household paper	Brown	Paper towels, napkins, brown paper bags— all fair game. You can even compost junk mail as long as you shred it.
Leaves	Brown	Collect dry leaves from your local public works department for free, if you don't have enough of your own. Shred them before composting so they don't mat.
Newspaper/ Cardboard	Brown	Separate corrugated cardboard layers and tear into small pieces or shred what you can so it breaks down more easily.
Straw/Hay	Brown	Straw generally has fewer weed seeds than hay, which makes it a better choice. To be safe, buy certified weed-free material.
Wood chips	Brown	Wood chips are high in carbon so toss in only a few, and mix in some green stuff to help neutralize them.
Woody branches	Brown	Chop branches into smaller pieces so they break down more easily, or ask for shredded branches from a local tree service.
Chicken manure	Green	Chicken manure is high in nitrogen. Add it to plants in small quantities only, and be sure to spread it evenly.

Material	Brown/Green	Notes
Coffee grounds/ Tea leaves	Green	You can compost the grounds, the filters, and the tea bags. All of it.
Composted cow/ horse/sheep/goat manure	Green	Manure amps up compost by adding beneficial bacteria. It's easy to find at gardening stores and a little goes a long way.
Food scraps	Green	Collect compostable food scraps in a covered bin under the sink or on the counter. (See "What to avoid.")
Garden waste	Green	Yellowing leaves, trimmings, and post-harvest plants are great sources of nutrients. Sort out any diseased plants.
Garden weeds	Green	Weeds are okay, unless they've gone to seed. To be safe, remove seed heads before adding any to your pile.
Grass clippings	Green	Add in thin layers to avoid clumping. Don't use if treated with herbicide.
Seaweed and kelp	Green	Soil needs certain vital trace nutrients and seaweed is a great source.
Egg shells	Neutral	A great source of calcium. To get the most out of them, crush before adding.
Greenhouse waste	Neutral	Tossing together potting soil and greenhouse debris is another good way to build soil.
Things to avoid		"Compostable" packaging and flatware, which need intense heat to break down. Bones, pet waste, human and pet hair, glossy coated paper, fish and meat scraps, large branches, synthetic fertilizer, weeds gone to seed.

it's usually sealed in plastic garbage bags. Without oxygen, the food undergoes anaerobic decomposition, producing methane, a greenhouse gas.

Methane traps about 20 times as much heat as carbon dioxide. Research from Project Drawdown, a climate-change mitigation project started by Paul Hawken, suggests that if we adopt composting on a global scale we could reduce emissions by 2.3 billion tons over the next 30 years.

Compost is made of food scraps and other natural debris, but without the plastic bags. Exposed to the soil and air, waste breaks down into simpler elements, like organic matter, fungi, and bacteria. When you shovel compost onto the soil around your plants, you're supplying nutrients and building a better soil structure. You're also fostering a lively community of the soil organisms that help lock in carbon.

I've made so much compost over the years I've become pretty casual about it. If I'm cleaning out a garden bed, I throw all the green garden waste (except weeds with seed pods) into the compost pile and top it with some straw or leaves, aiming for about half green and half brown. I throw in more brown material if it's slimy and smelly, and add more grass clippings and food scraps if it's breaking down too slowly. Too dry? I water my compost with a spinning sprinkler, leaving it on for about an hour at a time.

I used to surround my compost pile with big bales of hay to protect it from deer, but it still attracted squirrels and mice. You can more easily prevent pest invasions by using a box and lid made out of leftover lumber and wire screening, or a store-bought bin. The most popular store-bought bin is a tumbler, which allows you to toss in scraps and brown materials and easily spin the whole thing rather than having to turn your heap manually.

I prefer a stationary bin with three compartments because it gives me more control over the process. I can allow one compartment to sit and decompose while building new compost in the second compartment. I don't have to dig through a layer of decomposing food

THREE BIN

FINISHED COMPOST

BUILD YOUR PILE

STOCKPILE

If you have the room, build a three-bin composting station. The first bin allows a pile to sit and decompose. The second bin lets you build a new pile while you wait so you don't have to dig through a layer of decomposing food scraps to reach the compost at the bottom of the bin. You can use the third compartment to stockpile extra brown materials like small twigs, wood chips, or hay.

SINGLE BIN

If space or animals are an issue, a compact compost tumbler may be just the thing to churn out your black gold.

scraps to reach the compost at the bottom of the bin. I use the third compartment to hold extra brown materials like small twigs, wood chips, or hay I save up during the year. I seem to always have more of the green waste than the brown, so keeping extra brown stuff on hand makes it easier to achieve the right blend.

If you don't have enough room for a compost bin in your yard, no problem. You can buy an indoor composter that breaks down food scraps using a bacterial agent. Or bring in some worms to do the work. (Tip: learn what's involved in partnering up with worms before bringing them home!)

What can I use for mulch?

People often don't believe me when I tell them I spend less than 30 minutes a month weeding my garden. But it's true, thanks to all the mulching I've done.

Spending less time hunched over pulling weeds is just one reason to love mulch. Spreading it also helps trap moisture, so you won't need to water your plants as much, and it protects the soil, roots, and soil organisms against harsh weather elements.

You can use almost anything as a mulch. As a rule, I use mulches that break down over time because they add organic matter to the soil. For that reason, I stay away from plastic films. (See "Choose your mulch.")

What potting soil is best-suited to container gardening?

The most important quality to look for in potting soil is drainage. Light, fluffy soil that freely drains gives your plant access to moisture and room for roots to stretch out. Dense and soggy soil can stunt or kill your roots.

Commercial mixes can contain mined mineral rocks like perlite or vermiculite. Once these materials are treated with heat, they puff up like cheese doodles, making them fantastic at holding onto water. But the mining and heat treatments are energy intensive and release a lot of greenhouse gases.

CHOOSE YOUR MULCH

Mulch is a backyard carbon farmer's very good friend. Spreading it helps trap moisture so you won't need to water your plants as much. It fights weeds, so you spend less time hunched over pulling them out of the ground. It also protects soil, roots, and soil organisms against harsh weather elements, and adds organic matter to the soil. Almost anything can be used as a mulch, as long as it feeds and protects the soil. When I go out to mulch the garden, I pick materials that are inexpensive, easy to find, and make sense for the job at hand. Here's a quick breakdown of biodegradable mulching options.

Material	Best used for	Notes
Bark or wood chips	Pathways and other areas in the garden that see a lot of foot traffic since chips are sturdy and slow to decompose. Bark chips break down more easily than wood chips.	Use with green compost material or a high nitrogen fertilizer, such as blood meal, because bark/wood chips are high in carbon and microbe activity can create a localized nitrogen deficiency at the soil surface. A local tree service or utility company might be happy to give them away.
Coco fiber	Protecting seedlings in a greenhouse. Lightweight, easy to handle, and a great source of phosphorous.	The high nutrient content in coco fiber makes it potentially toxic to pets. It can also be expensive.
Dry grass	Adding nutrients, particularly nitrogen and phosphorous, to the soil.	Spread on lightly, in layers no greater than one-inch thick. Thicker clumps can rapidly decompose and overheat your plants. Remember not to use grass clippings treated with herbicides.
Gravel or pebbles	Improving drainage. Also protects cold-sensitive plants, since rocks absorb heat during the day and release it at night.	Pebbles can be messy and make it harder to dig, so reserve them for use in your planters or succulent garden.
Leaves	Just about anything. Crumbled leaves are a versatile source of mulch.	Shred wet leaves with a mower or crumble dry leaves. Whole dry leaves mat together and prevent water from reaching the soil.
Newspaper and cardboard	Creating a weed barrier before layering on compost and mulch.	Some inks and glues contain toxic chemicals, so avoid using glossy paper or coated cardboard.
Sawdust	Acid-loving perennials like blueberries.	Acidic and messy, so reserve for use with plants that thrive in acidic soils.
Straw or hay	Insulating perennials during the cold winter months.	Buy high-quality hay or straw ordinarily used for feed. Cheap hay or straw can be filled with weed seeds that can take over your garden. Straw generally has fewer weed seeds than hay.

Harvested peat moss is lightweight and porous, which means it's also good at holding on to air and water. But harvesting the peat moss from natural bogs damages native ecosystems. Even the most sustainably managed bog can take decades to bounce back, if it ever does. So look for potting mix free of peat moss, too.

Another option is to make your own. To prepare an environmentally friendly potting mix, measure out two gallons of coconut coir fiber, a waste product from processing coconuts that holds water. Mix it with two gallons of compost in a wheelbarrow. Add one gallon of sharp sand, which is commonly used to mix concrete, and a gallon of composted animal manure. Mix thoroughly, and you're done. If you don't use up all of your homemade potting mix in one go, store it in a dry place. I keep mine in a covered trash bin behind the shed.

My father, Wendell Berry, is often asked what a person should do if they can't farm. I have heard him answer that question hundreds of times by now, and he always does so with variations on the same theme.

"Grow something to eat," he says. "Raise a garden if you can." This will take you out of the money economy just a bit and mean learning to do something for yourself. Gardening, if done organically and regeneratively, involves surrendering to nature to some degree. The sun shines when it shines and rain comes when it comes. Soil responds beautifully to good care in ways that are to some extent explainable but mostly miraculous.

Gardening can teach us something of what we must know to survive. We have believed that what is good for us is good for the world and we have been wrong. We haven't thought deeply enough. We must change our thinking. We must acknowledge that much of the way of the world is a mystery. In growing something good to eat, we become participants in that mystery.

Can gardening help people understand farming better? This is an important question to keep in mind if we are to become a country of people who value good land use. The increasing interest in local, organic food has yet to change the prevailing culture of agriculture in this country. If we believe, and I do, that food is a cultural product, then we have a cultural problem on our hands.

A significant population seriously undertaking regenerative gardening might be just the shift that will finally change the culture, and agriculture.

—Mary Berry
Executive Director, The Berry Center
New Castle, Kentucky

PLANT YOUR CLIMATE VICTORY GARDEN

Before I set to work on the scrap of land that taught me so much about farming, I grew my first garden in Los Angeles. The tiny plot was fully exposed to the sun, so I chose to grow tomatoes and peppers, in addition to a sprawling trellis of passion fruit to create shade for the lettuce I planted. Every day I made sure my plants were watered, plucking the weeds as needed.

My garden responded by giving me a feast of plump tomatoes, crisp peppers, and juicy passion fruit, which I ate for the first time. All that sun and warm weather seduced me into thinking maybe I really did want to be a farmer. I mean, how hard could it be?

I called my parents to let them know. There was silence, then, in a whisper, "Are you sure?"

Absolutely!

Then came the move to Washington. Instead of sunny, warm LA, I had to deal with long, rainy winters and summers that were often scorching hot and dry, an extreme weather pattern unlike any

I had experienced before. The weather wasn't what the locals considered normal, either. While they were used to the rain, the summer droughts were getting longer. This was worrisome because in late summer we'd be blanketed in smoke from the wildfires that raged to the north and east of us, almost completely blocking the sun. It was eerie and, of course, very frightening.

A year later I was still trying to figure out what to plant and when. Spring was cool and wet, and the days were short. The summer weather was just the opposite: the sun didn't set until after 10:00 p.m., so the dry, hot days dragged on. What plants could possibly thrive in weather that swung between too much water and too little? Between not enough sun and way too much of it?

One late afternoon while I was pacing the farm, I observed which plants were thriving and which were most definitely not. I thrust my hand into the dirt to see if that could help explain it, and noted where it was sandy and where it was moist. For perhaps the first time, I studied the gentle mounds and occasional pockets that defined my land, and paid attention to where the wind ruffled the grasses and the bright afternoon sun was still shining.

That's when I took the step that proved to be the key to turning around our ailing farm: I drew a map. Sketching the outlines of the land, I marked the moist patches, the elevated areas that would drain quickly, and the spots where the sun beamed all afternoon. Then I got to work.

First I planted a border of currants and raspberries along the edge of my plot so the tall plants could act as a barrier to protect my crops from the wind. The sharp brambles would also help keep big pests like deer from helping themselves to the garden. I added a trellis of beans and planted heat-sensitive crops like spinach and lettuce in its shade. When I dug a new asparagus patch behind the greenhouse, I was careful to improve soil drainage with compost so the root crowns would survive the wet winter. I tore out the more demanding crops, like water-hungry celery, and planted additional beds of foolproof garlic and potatoes instead.

Strategic planting quickly turned around the farm. In fact, our farm was so successful, it eventually fed the entire community.

MAP YOUR SITE

You may be blessed with an acre or two, the way I was in Washington. More likely, your space resembles the garden I have now. When I arrived in New Hampshire I couldn't wait to get started. I wanted to build a carbon-sucking beauty of a Climate Victory Garden from the ground up *now!* Sadly, my new landlord wasn't sold on the idea. But my family lives nearby and it wasn't hard to persuade them to let me take a section of the yard for my new project.

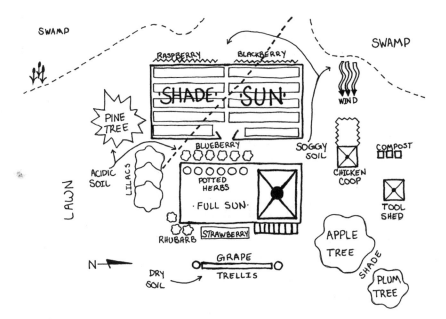

The first step to planning a successful Climate Victory Garden is to know your plot. Note where the sun falls throughout the day, the soil is soggy or compact, and in which direction the wind blows. Find plants that prefer sun, shade, or whatever type of soil you have, and place them where they're most likely to thrive.

I camped out under our old apple tree, and studied the little patch in New Hampshire as intently as I had my Northwest farmland, perhaps even more closely since lawn can cover up a multitude of sins. I observed where the soil was dry and gravelly, and where there was so much clay it was practically mud when it rained. Then I drew a map of my quirky plot, which has guided my choice of plants ever since.

Since my goal was to produce the richest, darkest patch of organic soil possible, my first thought was to pack it entirely with perennials. But I knew I'd dearly miss eating fresh-picked green beans, and filling up a salad bowl with my own lettuce and tomatoes. So I decided to plant mostly perennials, with a few annuals mixed in.

It's still a Climate Victory Garden. My Heritage raspberries help anchor the soil around my beans and lettuce, creating a safe place for healthy soil microorganisms to gather. By relying on regenerative techniques, like minimizing soil disturbance and composting regularly, I'm allowing organic matter to build. And if adding a few annuals makes gardening more rewarding, I'm all for it. Cultivating your own underground carbon sink can take time.

Two years into it, my once swampy dirt is now luscious dark brown soil and the strawberries, rhubarb, and other perennials I planted have almost completely taken over the garden. Yet all summer long, my salad bowl fills up with fresh lettuce, radishes, and tomatoes, just the way I like it.

CHOOSE RESILIENT PLANTS

Seed companies know where I live and, until recently, I shared my space with an alarmingly high stack of catalogs. One earthy-looking, pumpkin-colored seed catalog was all it took to suck up hours of my time. I'd fall hard for every pretty plant I saw, dreaming of a garden filled with Brandywine tomatoes and Burgess Buttercup squash.

But now I know better. I'm focused on the plants most likely to support a healthy soil ecology. Shallow-rooted annuals die every year, releasing their carbon back into the atmosphere as plant debris decomposes on the surface. For this reason, they don't store nearly as much carbon in the ground as perennials. So while I still leaf through my catalogs admiring the sunny annuals, the perennials section is what I zero in on. Many of them are pretty gorgeous, too.

To find the plants most likely to thrive and support your backyard carbon farming dreams, I suggest using the following guidelines.

Look to your map. Study your garden plot. If it's overshadowed by tall buildings, you'll need shade-loving plants. If it's predominantly sandy, you'll want plants that won't demand much water (and you'll have to keep pushing the compost so the soil becomes loamier).

Include a variety of plants, mostly perennials. In general, the more diverse your plantings, the healthier your garden will be. Different plants feed different communities of soil organisms, and planting a wide range invites them all. This makes your garden more resilient to droughts, floods, swings in temperature, and disease, especially if it contains sturdy perennials.

A variety of plants also provides shelter and food to lacewings, spiders, and other pest-eating bugs. Plants that bloom at different times improve the chances that birds, butterflies, and other pollinators will find plenty to eat. (For more information on how to attract pollinators, visit the website of the Xerces Society for Invertebrate Conservation.) Encouraging bugs and birds to visit can make your garden act more like a self-sustaining ecosystem, which means more reward with less effort.

Grow drought-tolerant plants. One climate-change reality is that drought conditions will only worsen. My Washington farm was located in the country's rainiest region, yet I struggled with summers so dry I was forced to irrigate. Planting perennials with roots long enough to find water deep underground will give your garden a fighting chance at staying green, despite climate challenges.

PERENNIAL PLANT CHARACTERISTICS

Knowing a plant's particular preferences makes it easier to pick the crops that will thrive.

Perennials	Name	Good groundcover	Drought-tolerant	Shade-tolerant	Good for containers
Vegetables	Asparagus		x		
	Artichoke				
	Radicchio			x	
	Rhubarb		x	x	
	Walking onion		x	x	x
	Watercress				x
	Tomato*		x	x	x
	Pepper*		x		
Fruits	Apple tree		x		
	Blackberry				
	Blueberry			x	x
	Currant			x	x
	Grape		x		
	Gogi berry		x		
	Huckleberry		x	x	
	Pear tree			x	
	Plum tree		x		
	Raspberry	x		x	
	Strawberry	x			x
Herbs	Chives		x	x	x
	Fennel				x
	Lavender		x	x	
	Lemon Balm	x	x	x	x
	Mint	x	x	x	x
	Oregano	x	x		x
	Parsley		x	x	x
	Rosemary	x	x		x
	Sage		x		x
	Thyme	x	x	x	x

* Tender perennials

Grows in acidic soil	Good for sandy soil	Good for clay soil	Spring harvest	Summer harvest	Fall harvest
	x		x		
				x	
	x	x		x	x
			x	x	
x	x			x	x
x			x		
	x			x	x
x	x			x	x
x	x			x	x
x	x				
x				x	
				x	
				x	
				x	
x	x				x
x	x			x	
x	x			x	
	x			x	
	x		x	x	x
		x	x	x	x
				x	
				x	x
				x	x
x	x			x	x
		x		x	x
	x	x	x	x	x
	x			x	x
	x			x	x

ANNUAL PLANT CHARACTERISTICS

Name	Good groundcover	Drought-tolerant	Shade-tolerant	Good for containers
Beans		x		x
Cabbage		x	x	
Carrot		x		x
Cucumber				
Garlic**		x		x
Kale			x	x
Lettuce			x	x
Peas			x	x
Potato**				
Radish			x	x
Spinach			x	x
Squash	x			

** Annuals that act like perennials if you leave a few tubers or cloves in the ground to propogate.

Grow plants you love to eat. I know this sounds obvious, but plant food crops you like and want to cook. What's the point of growing something you won't eat? If you plant what you love, gardening will seem less like a chore. Who cares about a little weeding when you know you'll soon sink your teeth into a crisp pepper?

TIME YOUR PLANTING

Even though I'm a seasoned farmer, I still struggle with timing. One winter, I was so excited about a new tomato variety that I started a tray inside as soon as the seeds arrived in my mailbox. Eight weeks later, they were still sitting under a grow light because it was too cold to move them outside. They grew spindly and weak while waiting for the fresh garden air.

Grows in acidic soil	Good for sandy soil	Good for clay soil	Spring harvest	Summer harvest	Fall harvest
X	X	X		X	
	X		X		X
X	X		X	X	X
X		X		X	
X	X			X	
X		X	X	X	X
	X	X	X	X	X
	X	X	X	X	
X	X			X	X
X	X		X	X	X
		X	X	X	X
X	X			X	X

Here's what I've learned about timing: wait for your soil to warm up before planting in it. Most seeds sown in cold soil won't sprout. Seedlings started too early indoors will get leggy, weak, and rootbound. And trees planted too soon can end up stunted and prone to disease.

Growers have traditionally relied on frost dates to time a spring planting. But predicting the last frost of the season is more difficult now that climate change is chewing up historic averages. Still, that data is all we have. I visit the Farmers' Almanac and National Weather Service websites for guidance. Both rely on information from the National Center for Environmental Information (NCEI), which gives average spring dates when the likelihood of frost has passed.

Even if you follow the last frost dates precisely, there's still the small chance of a late season frost. I hedge my bets against a cold snap by bringing potted plants indoors at night or covering them with light fabric until I'm sure spring is really here.

START YOUR PLANTS

You have three choices when it comes to starting plants: planting seeds or cuttings in an indoor pot, putting seeds or cuttings directly in the ground, or buying plants from a nursery. I tend to use the first option because I'm always anxious to get planting, and you never know what kind of weather spring will bring. But choose whatever works for you.

Planting in the ground

Seeding in the ground is the most straightforward way to start a garden and it frees up indoor space for stuff other than grow lights, heating mats, and pots—things like couches and lamps. But there are risks. You're betting your tender shoots won't freeze in a late blast of frost or drown in a pile of spring mud. Pests love to munch on seedlings, particularly when they're at their most tender. And newly planted seeds need to be consistently moist to sprout evenly, so you'll have to stick around to water them or install irrigation.

To prep your patch, first clear it of weeds, then shovel on a pile of bagged or homemade compost every few feet and spread it evenly with a rake to cover the surface of your garden. (Unless you made new, compost-filled beds or your garden was freshly composted in the spring, in which case you can skip this step.)

Prep the soil by loosening and aerating it to allow water and air to percolate in. I use a broadfork, a heavy U shaped tool with metal tines and a base, which allows me to work over the ground while preserving the underground community of soil critters. Think of it as a soil-friendly rototiller.

First, drive the broadfork into the soil, with the slightly curved tines pointing up. Next, step on the base of the U and wiggle it so the tines go deep into the soil. Step off the broad fork and pull the handle towards you and down, driving the tines up towards the surface of the soil. Notice how this opens up deep pockets of air. To continue down your bed, take a step backwards, and start the process all over again. You'll work the soil moving backwards in one to two foot sections.

Equipment: Trowel, bamboo stake or stick

Drop in seeds. A good rule of thumb is to plant seeds as deep as they are wide and space them so when plants mature they have plenty of room. This means pushing in large seeds like squash and beans about an inch deep before pinching the soil closed. For smaller seeds, like beets and carrots, you can save time by dragging a bamboo stake or trowel through the soil and making a shallow one-eighth-inch furrow. Drop in seeds and cover with a thin layer of soil. For really tiny seeds, like most herbs and greens, sprinkle them on top of the soil, cover gently, and pat them down. Water your seeds lightly to avoid washing them away.

I tend to plant more densely than is generally recommended on seed packets because I'd rather take out any extra plants once they grow than wish I'd planted more.

Plant cuttings. Perennials like berry bushes and some herbs can take too long to grow from seed. You can get around that by planting cuttings, which are bits of roots and branches from mature plants. The benefit of using cuttings is that slow-growing perennials will get bigger more quickly.

Choose stems or branches that look healthy and robust and show no visible signs of disease. Make sure your cutting has at least a few nodes, or tiny notches, where new leaves will push out. Place your cutting in the ground along with some of your favorite potting mix. Bury the stem at least four inches deep, cut side down. If it's top heavy or unstable, push it deeper. To speed up the rooting process, dip cut ends into willow extract, which promotes new root growth.

Depending on the plant, it can take anywhere from one to six months for your cuttings to take root and grow. You'll know it's firmly rooted if you gently tug on the top of the stem and the cutting stays put, or shoots out new signs of growth, like buds or leaves.

Planting indoors first

I like starting my plants inside while waiting for the ground to get warm and dry. Fussing over them in my controlled indoor environment makes it more likely my seeds will sprout. Starting seedlings inside also gives my warm-season crops, like tomatoes and peppers, a head start on ripening before the time is up on New Hampshire's short growing season.

Equipment: Seed flats or biodegradable pots, potting soil, heat mat, grow light

Choose your pots. The most efficient way to plant multiple seeds, in terms of time and space, is to sow them in cell flats or a seed tray. Cell flats are plastic containers separated into tiny pockets, each about one inch by one inch. One flat can hold anywhere from 6 to 200 plants. Once your seeds sprout, you'll have to transfer them into larger pots or they won't develop healthy roots. If you have the indoor space, you can plant directly into bigger pots.

When choosing pots, consider biodegradable materials like cow manure, paper pulp, and coconut coir fiber. With these pots, your seedlings never have to experience the shock of being transplanted from pot into ground. (As with any living thing, seedlings can become traumatized.) You simply plant the whole container, adding organic matter to the soil while keeping plastic out of landfills.

Plant your seeds. Fill your pots or flats with potting soil, bagged or homemade. Then insert at least two seeds per cell or pot to improve your odds of getting at least one to germinate. Seed packets generally offer instructions on how deep to plant them. Moisten the soil without soaking it. When seedlings have sprouted two leaves, thin or remove the extra plant to give the healthiest one room to grow.

Keep seeds warm. Set your indoor plants on a heat mat if your home tends to run cold. Seeds need warm soil to sprout, unless they're cool-season crops like kale and spinach. Starting seeds in warm soil also increases a sprout's vigor and resilience; weak sprouts tend to grow into frail plants. Keep your heat mat on 24 hours a day until your seeds sprout.

Using a heat mat will dry out the soil quickly, especially if you're planting in tiny one-inch cells, so water your seeds frequently. If you have to leave the house for a few days, fitting little plastic domes over your cell flats can keep the moisture from evaporating. It's like creating a tabletop greenhouse.

Give them light. Set your baby plants on a sunny windowsill. If you don't get much sun, invest in a grow light, which is easy to find online or at most gardening centers. I prefer LED grow lights because they use less energy than fluorescent bulbs and don't get too hot, which means I can leave them on without worrying when I'm out of the house. Set up your light with a timer to mimic day and night, and you have one less thing to think about. An indication your seedlings are light deprived is if they become leggy with long, bending stems.

Transplant your seedlings (carefully). Your new plants are ready for the big move outdoors once they've sprouted at least two or three leaves. Still, take it slow. Keep them inside if the weather is too cold. Seedlings accustomed to a sheltered life indoors need to be introduced gradually to the outdoors or they won't thrive in their new environment.

Wait for a nice sunny day before bringing your young plants outside for the first time. Let your coddled seedlings bask, but bring them in before nightfall. Do this for about a week to acclimate your plants.

Before transplanting, you want the soil in your pot to be moist but not soggy so the plant slides out easily and the roots hang on to clumps of soil. I generally presoak the soil or wait to plant until after a good rain. Note that transplanting potted plants on cloudy or rainy days is less stressful for them.

Once your plants are ready, dig a hole in your garden a little wider than the pot and just as deep. Make a V with your index and middle fingers and place it on either side of the seedling. Turn the pot upside down and, using your fingers to prevent the plant from falling out, tap the bottom of the pot and gently lift. If the seedling doesn't easily slide out, try squeezing the sides of the pot and gently shake it out. You can skip this step if you're using biodegradable pots.

Once the seedling is out, place it in the hole. If your plant has been sitting for a while it might have become rootbound. A sign plants are rootbound is if you see roots growing out the bottom of the pot. In this case, it's good to break up the roots a little before lowering them into the hole so they can spread out.Tear off the bits of roots poking out of the pot or use scissors to snip them away.

Then, fill in the hole with soil and press down gently so the roots come into contact with the ground. Water the new seedling around the base, avoiding the leaves so they're less likely to develop fungus or mold. Always add mulch to the base of new plants to help the soil stay moist and slightly cooler, and to ease the transition. Consider protecting your new seedlings from the sun by covering them with upside-down baskets or burlap propped up with sticks, until they adjust to their new environment.

Water your plants

After your new plants and seeds are in the ground they need regular watering—daily if possible but a few times a week at minimum. You can ease off to once or twice a week after they become established.

Deep waterings encourage root growth, which helps your plants cope with dry periods, so aim to give your perennials a weekly soak. Annuals need more frequent watering because of their shallow roots. Try to give them up to a half–inch of water, twice a week. Plants grown in containers need more watering, as often as once a day during the hottest summer months. Plants in larger pots need less watering than those in smaller ones.

QUESTIONS

How can I find plants that grow well where I live?

Your first step is to figure out which gardening climate zone you live in. Consult the Hardiness Zone Map, an interactive map produced by the US Department of Agriculture (USDA) that divides the country into 11 separate planting zones and tracks how cold it gets in each one. Another source is a map produced by the National Oceanic and Atmospheric Administration (NOAA), which also reports on the coldest temperature for each US location. Although factors other than temperature affect the ability of a plant to survive —including light, precipitation, and the quality of the soil— knowing the temperature below which a plant will not survive is certainly helpful.

Once you've identified your zone, go online to Farmers' Almanac to generate a list of the plants most likely to thrive in your neighborhood, or visit your local gardening supply store and ask the experts what grows well. Be sure to investigate regionally compatible varieties. More than 300 types of thyme exist, for example, and each one is adapted to a certain climate. Some are well suited to the hot, dry summers of the Southwest, and others do better in the cooler Midwest; certain varieties thrive better in wet soil, while others grow at high elevations with poor soil, gale force winds, and drought. Your local garden store expert should know which varieties are worth your time.

Not incidentally, both the USDA and NOAA hardiness maps find that warmer zones are shifting northward. My own plant hardiness zone has changed from a 5b, where temperatures drop below −10 degrees in winter, to a 6a, where minimum temperatures hover between −5 and −10 degrees. This means I can now grow varieties of grapes that used to survive only in more temperate climates. I can also keep certain herbs, like lavender, in the ground during the winter instead of digging them up each fall to protect them.

Still more evidence that the climate crisis isn't something that's coming. It's here.

I have a tiny garden. How do I maximize my space?

You don't need a lot of space to start a garden, especially if you follow the golden rule of small-space gardening: choose naturally climbing crops, like runner beans, grapes, and cherry tomatoes. Growing up increases your yield and makes harvesting easier. I also happen to love the way vertical gardens look.

Another way to squeeze more out of your small space is to practice succession planting, which means planting more than one crop in a single space throughout the season. I plant early-season radishes outside, for example, while waiting for my warm-season crops like peppers and tomatoes to grow inside. Once I harvest the radishes, I pop the peppers and tomatoes in their place.

In addition to making efficient use of space, succession planting is a way to make sure your ground is never bare. Keeping roots in the ground is a good way to enhance soil fertility and preserve topsoil, which in turn increases your soil's carbon-storing capacity.

Can I practice backyard carbon farming if I only have pots to plant in?

As you might guess, growing food in pots does not have the same carbon-capturing power as planting in the ground. But you can enjoy the same carbon-saving advantages that all regenerative gardeners enjoy, no matter the size of the plot.

Growing your own food, even in small amounts, means you might make fewer trips to the grocery store and pay more attention to the seasonality of food. It may make you more likely to support farmers who embrace no-till, cover-cropping, and composting practices. And more willing to get behind politicians taking bold measures to combat climate change, protect the environment, and promote good food practices.

Apart from all that, homegrown food is delicious.

Mix together plants of varying heights and harvest times to take advantage of every square inch of garden, attract pollinators and other beneficial bugs, and improve resilience overall.

You can grow food regeneratively in just about anything that holds soil. Add compost or organic potting soil to your container to improve resilience and conserve moisture. Plant perennials in a big pot if you want to create your own healthy soil ecosystem. Soil organisms like worms and bacteria will find their way in through drainage holes and perform the same great carbon-capturing work they do in the ground—just on a smaller scale.

When my wife and I took over my in-laws' 1,800-acre farm in North Dakota in 1993, we had about 1,000 acres of spring wheat, oats, and barley. We also had very poor topsoil. It was made up of 1.7 percent organic matter and absorbed a scant half-inch of rainfall per hour. So we decided to diversify our crops and go zero-till.

In 1994, we added cereal rye, winter triticale (a hybrid cross between wheat and rye), field peas, and hairy vetch to the cash crop rotation. Four years later, we added deeply rooted, soil-building cover crops, like sorghum-sudangrass and cowpeas. We also introduced 150 cow and calf pairs; proper, sustainable grazing techniques can lead to high levels of carbon being cycled out of the atmosphere, and back into the soil.

Today we have a plot of land that is 11 percent organic matter, and soil that can absorb more than 30 inches of rainfall an hour. We are producing more nutrient-dense food at a lower cost than the conventional production model, and our ranch, which has grown to 5,000 acres, is profitable every year. We do all this without taking any government subsidies of any type. We have done this without using synthetic fertilizers, pesticides, or fungicides. We did this simply by following the principles of nature.

Yes, we can feed the world. We can do it in a way that regenerates our resources thereby healing our farms, families, and communities. Gardeners, too, can have a positive or negative impact on our ecosystem. If you till the soil or apply synthetic fertilizers and pesticides, not only will you lower the nutrient density of the food you're producing but those compounds will end up polluting our watersheds and producing toxins that can poison communities and wildlife alike.

Each of us can have a significant positive impact on our resources, our environment, and our health. Make the decision to support regenerative growing. Your health will benefit, your children and grandchildren's health will benefit, and your environment will benefit, too.

—Gabe Brown
Brown's Ranch
Bismarck, North Dakota

STARTER PLANTS FOR BACKYARD CARBON FARMERS

I'm often asked how to maximize our impact as backyard carbon farmers. Planting perennials is one sure way to do it. They have deep roots that stay put, providing a safe haven for carbon capturing soil organisms. They return year after year so you only have to plant them once. And, my favorite, they conserve underground resources, using water and nutrients only as needed, because they're in it for the long haul.

Annuals, by contrast, are greedy. They grow quickly and die within one growing season, sucking up any nutrients and water their roots can find, whether they need it or not, and releasing carbon back into the air when they die and decompose on the soil's surface. They have to be planted every year, which means seasonal digging that disrupts communities of the soil organisms we carbon farmers work so hard to cultivate, and they can't store nearly the amount of carbon that perennials can.

But becoming a backyard carbon farmer doesn't mean you have to ditch your favorites entirely. If you love growing delicious annuals, like peas, spinach, and squash, then plant a few. You can grow anything using a soil-first approach. Heaping on compost and keeping roots in the ground after harvest are just a couple of ways to enhance any plant's regenerative effect.

That said, to get the most out of your Climate Victory Garden, pack as many perennials into it as you can.

In the plant guide that follows, I include seven perennials that are either particularly easy to grow or true carbon champions (fruit trees!). Tucked in here as well are tomatoes and peppers because I can't imagine a garden without them. They're considered tender perennials, which can survive more than one season if you bring them inside when it turns cold. I also list 12 popular backyard annuals with suggestions on how to maximize their carbon capturing impact.

A more complete set of perennials can be found in *Growing Perennial Foods*, the companion to this book. It details how to grow 34 perennial herbs, fruits, and vegetables, and includes recipes, too.

STARTER PERENNIALS

BLACKBERRY

Inviting hungry birds into the garden is a natural way to control pests. Bird feeders are one way to draw them in, but a lot of insect-loving birds also eat fruit. Blackberries produce so much fruit you won't mind sharing them with helpful birds.

Varieties: Blackberries come in more than 300 varieties. Some form impenetrable thorny thickets, while others sprawl as groundcover. Since the fruit is highly adaptable, it's easy to find varieties that will grow almost anywhere.

WHERE IT THRIVES

Regional compatibility: Blackberries do well in most soil types, making them among the easiest fruits to grow. Certain varieties, like the Himalayan blackberry, grow so vigorously they're considered an invasive weed in some areas. Before planting any berries, consult your local extension office on which varieties are best for your region so you don't contribute to the spread of invasive plants.

Optimal sun and shade: You'll get the greatest number of berries if you plant bushes in full sun.

Resilience: Blackberries do fairly well in both cold and warm climates. But they don't do well in drought, because they need water to produce good fruit, and soil that's too wet will stunt their growth. The key to growing resilient berries is to plant them in well-drained soil if you live in a wet, rainy climate and give them a yearly dose of compost if you live in a hot, dry climate.

PLANTING

Best time of year: Plant nursery-grown bushes or rooted cuttings in the spring after the last frost or in the fall before winter settles in.

Best way to plant: To produce your own cutting, snip up to eight inches of growth from a healthy plant. It's best to do this in the fall when the plant starts dropping leaves. Cuttings need a cold treatment, about three weeks in a refrigerator, before they're ready to be planted in a pot with well-draining soil or right into the ground.

If you don't want to bother with a cold treatment, try planting pieces of roots. Snip a two-inch piece of root from a mature plant and dig it into the ground in the spring. Monitor the plant for new growth and keep it well watered until the leaves grow back.

GROWING

The area around my house is filled with blackberry brambles thanks to birds feasting on them and dropping seeds on flyovers. I remove most of the bushes just after they sprout, when the roots are still weak and easy to yank. The ones left over make up a garden perimeter that helps keep out the deer, gophers, and groundhogs.

Blackberries begin bearing fruit in their second year. After a long, hollow stem (known as a cane) fruits, it dies. That's one reason this shrub needs pruning at the end of each summer. Pruning is also the only way to manage the growth of this often unruly plant.

Cut the fruit-bearing canes all the way down to the base, leaving four of the strongest and healthiest canes. This gives any new growth enough space and sunlight to ripen the berries. If you want a natural-looking but less productive bramble, prune less often and allow it to mound up and spread out.

CHALLENGES

Blackberries can quickly take over a yard so if you're working with a small space, confine them to pots, raised beds, or containers. If you do plant them in the ground, rely on mulching to curb weed growth rather than weeding these prickly bushes yourself.

HARVEST

Pick your berries when they're deep black, preferably while dressed in long sleeves and pants you don't mind getting torn. Bring a pail to collect the berries, but don't stack too many on top of each other or you'll squash the ones on the bottom. Blackberries don't last long after they've been plucked, so try to eat them within three or four days.

CURRANT

Currants are easy to grow, mature quickly, and can produce fruit for up to 15 years. They have a make-you-pucker sourness that some people love and others, well, don't.

Varieties: These berries come in a range of types that vary in tartness. White currants are the sweetest, red currants are very tart, and black currants have a deep, earthy taste that some say resembles black tea.

WHERE IT THRIVES

Regional compatibility: Currants are exceptionally cold hardy, which makes them a great choice for northern growers.

Optimal sun and shade: Currants aren't picky when it comes to sunlight. You can plant them in full sun or partial shade. In warm climates, they benefit from dappled shade throughout the day, particularly in the afternoon. This helps prevent the ripening fruits from getting scorched by the sun.

Resilience: These plants adapt well to the cold, even in winter temperatures as low as −40 degrees. They are less forgiving of extremely hot or dry conditions; in hot climates, currants do better when they get sunlight from the north and have shade to the south.

PLANTING

Best time of year: Plant in the early spring or fall to escape the heat.

Best way to plant: When I started a hedgerow of currants a few years back, all I had to do was take a few branch cuttings from a neighbor and plant them in the ground, cut side down. I had baby currant plants by the end of the first summer, and they produced fruit the very next year.

Cut sprigs in the early spring from branches at least a year old. Dip the cut end of each cutting into willow extract. While roots can grow on their own, it can take a long time; willow extract speeds up the process so you'll be able to transplant your new shrubs into your fall garden. Place the cuttings in a pot or directly into the ground, cut side down, and push your cuttings into the soil at least four inches deep. When you move potted cuttings into the garden give them room by planting each five feet apart. They'll quickly fill the space.

GROWING

Currants are really easy to grow. The only real problem is how popular they are with deer, mice, birds, and rabbits. I've even caught my farm dog, Nimbus, snacking on low-hanging berries. If your yard gets a lot of traffic from animals and birds, you may want to drape your plants with netting until it's harvest time. (After you've picked your berries, roll up the netting and save it for next year.)

As they grow, be sure to prune your bushes or they'll get out of control (unless that's what you want). Cutting out broken branches, and old ones that have stopped flowering, minimizes the risk of disease and promotes new growth and healthy berries. For the best harvest, aim to have 6 to 12 healthy branches on every plant, and try to keep branches of different ages. For example, my currant plants have a few branches of first year growth, second year growth, and third year growth. I always cut out the older, less productive, four-year-old branches.

CHALLENGES

It's best not to plant currants, particularly black currants, near groves of white pine. This tree can carry white pine blister rust, a harmful fungus that can devastate your shrubs. Currants can also serve as an alternative host for the fungus. Some states have outlawed planting currants to keep pine forests safe from the spread of this disease, so check to see whether they're allowed where you live.

Currant leaves are the perfect hideout for aphids, which like to suck out the sugars found in leaves. Small populations won't harm plants, but large numbers may weaken them. If you notice leaves starting to curl, spray the tiny bugs with an insecticidal soap to keep the population from exploding.

HARVEST

Currants taste best when they're allowed to fully ripen on the shrub. The tart berries grow in clusters like grapes, so you can pick them one by one as they ripen or just snip the main stem when most of the berries are ready. The top berries in the cluster ripen earlier than the bottom ones. Keep picked berries out of the sun.

FRUIT TREES

Planting trees is the best way to maximize the carbon-storing potential of your garden. The average tree can absorb as much as 48 pounds of carbon dioxide per year and will have sequestered about 1 ton of carbon dioxide by the time it reaches 40 years old.

Varieties: Far too many fruit trees exist to highlight in this book, so I'll leave you with my two favorites. Pome fruits, like apples, pears and quince, have a core made of several seeds. These trees need a winter chill period to stay productive. Sunny, warm areas in the summer and good shelter from strong winds are best for pome fruit trees.

Stone fruits, like apricots, cherries, nectarines, and plums, have a hard central pit and grow best in sunny and sheltered climates. But plenty of varieties are bred to handle colder areas, and planting a tree in a container and moving it to a sheltered spot for the winter allows you to grow just about anything, anywhere.

I recommend buying bare-root trees that are grown in the ground and dug up so their roots are not constrained by a tiny pot. Bare-root trees adjust more quickly to native backyard soil compared to trees transplanted from a pot. Potted trees also tend to be rootbound, which makes it harder for them to stretch out their roots and grow once they're planted in the ground. Bare-root trees generally cost less so you can fill your garden with more than just one if you're on a budget.

Trees come in three general sizes: large, medium, and small. Unless you have a big yard, you'll want to pass on a large, full-size tree, which requires a lot of maintenance, pruning, and watering. Medium, or semi-dwarf, trees are three-quarters the size of regular ones. And small, dwarf trees grow to a third their normal size and fit nicely in large containers. Most fruit trees, from apples to peaches, are available in all three sizes.

WHERE THEY THRIVE

Regional compatibility: You can't grow apricots on a windy mountaintop or apples in the desert, but for every region there is a fruit tree that will thrive.

Optimal sun and shade: For the best harvest, the general rule of thumb is to plant trees where they'll get full sun at least six hours a day.

Resilience: Once in-ground trees mature, they pretty much take care of themselves because their roots are deep enough to find the water and nutrients hidden underground. But long dry seasons can take a toll on the quality and quantity of fruit, and waterlogged soils can rot roots, slowly killing your tree.

PLANTING

Best time of year: The optimal time to plant fruit trees is early spring just before the buds burst or in the fall after the leaves drop. Both seasons are a prime time for root growth. Planting trees in the summer is okay, but they'll need more water to deal with the heat stress.

Best way to plant: Find a location that isn't too damp or waterlogged. When trees are stuck in a big puddle for too long, the roots will rot and decay.

Dig a hole wider than the tree's rootball but not as deep. You want the roots to fit within the hole's diameter when straightened out so they don't twist around one another and choke the tree. If you find yourself with soggy soil, dig your hole a little deeper and add some rocks to the bottom of the hole, making a mound. Place your tree on top of the mound, spreading the roots down the side. This keeps your tree out of any puddles that might collect in the soil after a rain.

Most fruit trees are sold as grafts, meaning two parts of different trees are stuck together: the scion (a piece of branch) and the rootstock (a piece of root). Set the tree in the hole, making sure the graft scar, where the scion wood meets the root stock, is six inches above the soil line. If you bury the scar, the tree won't grow properly, and the scar could get infected.

Fill in the rest of the hole with an equal mixture of native soil and compost. When I dig a tree hole, I place the displaced soil in a wheelbarrow primed with compost so it's well mixed when I pour it back in. If you're planting more than one tree, give each a wide berth so they don't compete for water as they mature.

GROWING

Some trees can pollinate and bear fruit all by themselves. Apricots, peaches, nectarines, and sour cherries are among the self-pollinating champions. Other fruit trees, like apples, plums, and pears, need to cross-pollinate with trees that blossom at the same time so honey bees and other pollinators can fertilize them. If you're planting a cross-pollinating species, you'll need to plant more than one tree.

Prune your trees occasionally to limit their size and promote fruit production. Don't cut large branches flush with the trunk or main stem; you may think it looks neater this way but it's harder for the tree to heal from the trauma. Instead, leave a little piece of the branch sticking out and prune to the branch collar, that place where the branch flares out before it attaches to the trunk. This helps prevent rot from entering the trunk.

CHALLENGES

Tree branches overloaded with fruit can break, so thin out or remove the baby fruit leaving three to six inches between them. Be on the alert for suckers, which are long, straight branches that grow from a root stock to produce another, smaller tree. Remove them as soon as possible because they zap energy from the tree, choking its supply of water and nutrients.

Soft fruit makes the trees vulnerable to pests. Fruit-tree borers, aphids, fruit-tree leafrollers, fruit flies, and thrips—all of them prey on fruit trees. Various organic treatments that can safely remove pests from trees without harming the fruit include insecticidal soaps, neem oil, a vegetable oil extracted from the neem tree, and Bacillus thuringiensis (Bt), a soil-borne bacteria. (See "Common diseases and organic controls," page 144.)

HARVEST

Pick fruit as it ripens. To test for ripeness, taste a sample—for most fruit, if it's sweet, it's ready. If it's even a little bit astringent and sucks moisture from your mouth, wait a little longer to harvest. The fruit can remain on the tree for weeks without going bad, so don't fret if you harvest erratically. Pears are an exception because they ripen from the inside out, and it's rare you can eat them right off the tree.

HERBS

Herbs are about as accommodating as garden plants get. Once established, they'll return year after year with very little effort on your part. The nearly bulletproof herbs listed here are great garden companions because their pungent aroma helps deter pests while their dainty flowers attract pollinators. If you're nervous about ripping out your lawn or just don't have the space for a garden, planting herbs in containers is a nice compromise.

Varieties: Easy herbs to grow include chives, mint, lemon balm, oregano, sage, thyme, and rosemary.

WHERE THEY THRIVE

Regional compatibility: Some herbs like rosemary, won't survive a cold snap unless you bring them inside for the winter. You can keep almost any herb as a perennial if you shelter it from freezing cold, which is why I keep many of them in pots. Another option is to just let the plants go to seed in the fall; they'll sprout on their own the following spring.

Optimal sun and shade: Herbs can handle lots of sun; in fact, they prefer it.

Resilience: Herbs put up with bad weather and tend to be drought-tolerant. They grow equally well in outdoor gardens and indoor pots.

PLANTING

Best time of year: Plant herbs in the spring and early summer.

Best way to plant: Growing herbs from seed is a challenge because they're slow to sprout. I prefer picking up seedlings or fresh plants at my local farmers market and transplanting them into the ground. You can also grow many herbs from cuttings taken from mature plants.

To turn one plant into many, cut off a few four-inch unflowered stems. Trim the ends and place them in a glass of water, changing it every week to keep it fresh. New roots will sprout in about a week if it's warm enough. Plant your cuttings outdoors once the roots are at least a half-inch long.

GROWING

Most herbs grow well in somewhat coarse and sandy soil, which means you won't be pressured to produce the loamy, organically rich soil most other plants prefer in your first year of gardening.

To keep herbs from getting too leggy, snip off the tips of the stems to encourage outward instead of upward growth. You can trim back an established plant a couple of times during the growing season. A general rule of thumb is to never cut away more than a third of any plant in one season.

Herbs can start losing their flavor as plants get old, so thin out the older plants that have mostly brown, woody stems. Since many herbs self-seed prolifically, new plants will quickly make up for the loss.

In cooler climates, lay a bed of straw around the base of the plants once the soil is frozen to help them survive the winter. Come spring, remove the mulch and the soil will warm up more quickly.

CHALLENGES

Most herbs do not like wet feet. Soggy soil promotes fungal diseases like fusarium root rot or rusts that can kill your plants. Good drainage is key to keeping your herbs disease-free and alive throughout cold winters.

HARVEST

Harvest your herbs when stems are about eight inches tall. The more frequently you pick them, the faster your plant will grow. Herb flavors peak just before the plant flowers. Extend peak flavor by pinching off the flowers and allowing the plant to focus on growing leaves. Keep fresh clippings in a cup of water on your kitchen counter for up to a week. You'll love how the strong aroma fills your home.

RHUBARB

Rhubarb is a hardy plant thanks to its long taproot, so hold off on harvesting the stalks for the first year after planting to give it enough time to store energy below ground. The stronger the root, the better the vegetable will withstand drought and cold snaps.

Varieties: Choose your rhubarb based on how you want to prepare it. Some varieties, like Canadian red, are best for pies, while the pink-stalked Sunrise is better for canning and freezing. Your local garden center should be helpful in directing you to the rhubarb you want.

WHERE IT THRIVES

Regional compatibility: For rhubarb to grow, it first needs to be exposed to cold weather so it does best in cool regions like New England and the Midwest. In warm climates where winter temperatures rarely fall below 40 degrees, this plant is often grown as an annual.

Optimal sun and shade: Full sun is rhubarb's preference in moderate to cool regions. Partial shade is better for growth and flavor in warm climates.

Resilience: This vegetable benefits from occasional cold snaps and can withstand brief periods of drought. What rhubarb doesn't like is soggy soil and a lot of rain; waterlogged rhubarb can become stunted.

PLANTING

Best time of year: Plant rhubarb in the spring or fall. Spring is best if you live in a region with cold winters, while fall is better if you live in a warm area.

Best way to plant: Rhubarb is typically grown from crowns, which look like root stubs. Start by digging a hole about one foot by one foot. Before planting your crowns, work in one part compost to two parts soil. Make sure the roots are buried two to four inches beneath the soil line and at least four feet apart. Your rhubarb and its lush foliage will eventually take up a lot of space.

GROWING

Once rhubarb is established, it grows quickly and requires little tending. In fact, rhubarb is so resilient it's hard to get rid of, even when you hack it back repeatedly.

This low-maintenance vegetable does best when divided every five years or so. Otherwise, it eventually chokes itself out and loses vigor—which, granted, can be a good thing. Lift each crown with a pitchfork, split it into three or four pieces, and replant them around the garden. If you already have enough rhubarb, share the extra plants with neighbors.

CHALLENGES

Rhubarb is susceptible to crown rot. To prevent this, plant it in well-drained soil or on a mound. Once plants are infected, it's impossible to get rid of the disease; you'll have to dig up your compromised crowns and throw them out. Don't replant rhubarb in the same spot once this occurs or it could happen again.

HARVEST

Resist harvesting rhubarb for the first year so it has a chance to mature and develop its root system. Rhubarb stalks can be harvested when they're between 12 and 18 inches long. Mature rhubarb has a harvest period lasting about two months.

To harvest, twist and pull the stalk at the base or simply cut it with a harvesting knife. If you remove all the leaves, rhubarb will struggle to regrow the next season, so leave two to three stalks on each plant.

STRAWBERRY

Strawberries are low growing and make a wonderful groundcover that protects the soil. Leave older plants in the ground and they may be less productive but you'll have a low-maintenance, free-spreading fruit that is good for the earth.

Varieties: Strawberries are not just a springtime crop. You can find varieties that produce multiple harvests throughout the spring and summer. June-bearing strawberries produce one large crop in the spring. Day-neutral strawberries produce smaller quantities of fruit throughout the spring and summer, no matter how much daylight they get. Everbearing strawberries yield two or three crops of berries during the growing season.

WHERE IT THRIVES

Regional compatibility: Strawberries thrive in almost every climate, although where temperatures drop below 20 degrees it can be hard to grow them as perennials.

Optimal sun and shade: Strawberries love the sun, so give it to them.

Resilience: Strawberries need rain or regular watering to produce fruit, so they're not very drought-tolerant. Optimal fruit-ripening temperature is between 60 and 80 degrees.

PLANTING

Best time of year: Plant in the spring if you have harsh winters. If you have mild, frost-free winters, plant in the late fall.

Best way to plant: Strawberries send out runners, baby plants that branch out of the main plant from a thin stem connected to the roots. You can snip off baby plants and place them in the soil, pressing them down so they don't blow away, and they'll root on their own. If you have neighbors with an established strawberry patch, ask for a few runners to start your own. Otherwise, buy a few strawberry plants. Within a few seasons, you'll have your own full patch.

GROWING

If you live in a northern climate, keep very young strawberries inside in pots for the winter and move them into the ground come spring. In warm southern climates, all they need to survive the winter is a layer of mulch; they'll grow into adult plants the following summer.

CHALLENGES

Nobody can resist the sweet flesh of strawberries, or so it can seem. Plant your berries among leafy plants, like lettuce to hide the ripening fruit from hungry birds. Another way to hide them is under straw mulch. Straw also prevents the berries from touching the ground and becoming snacks for pests like wood bugs or slugs.

HARVEST

Eating a warm strawberry fresh from the garden never gets old—and that really is the best way to enjoy them because they lose flavor rapidly. Harvest strawberries when they're bright red by cutting or snapping the stems with your fingers. If you notice white areas on a berry, rotate the fruit so the pale side faces the sun. It will fully ripen in a day or two. I check my patch daily once the berries start reddening so I can snatch up the ripe ones before the birds and bugs get them.

WALKING ONION

This vigorous plant, also known as tree onion or topset onion, grows well in both very cold and very warm places. Its hassle-free nature makes it a great starter plant for new gardeners, plus you get to see the onions "walk" across the garden thanks to tiny bulbs called topsets at the top of the plant.

Varieties: The most common variety is the Egyptian walking onion, but you can also find Merceron Red Catawissa and Fleener's Topsetting onion in some seed catalogs.

WHERE IT THRIVES

Regional compatibility: Walking onions are extremely hardy and can withstand very cold winters. I've harvested bulbs in the dead of winter and, while they've lost their snap, the thawed bulbs taste just fine. The plant does okay in warm climates but doesn't fare well in hot and humid summers. Instead of tasty bulbs at the top of the plant, you might get flowers that go to seed instead.

Optimal sun and shade: Walking onions thrive with six hours of full sun a day. In hotter regions, afternoon shade helps prevent heat stress.

Resilience: Walking onions are drought-tolerant and, once established, need no help flourishing. In dry conditions, the bulb at the base of the plant will be smaller and more pungent but delicious nonetheless.

PLANTING

Best time of year: Plant walking onions anytime after the ground has thawed, and before the first fall frost.

Best way to plant: Walking onions grow best from topsets, which are this plant's version of a clove (like garlic) you pop in the ground.

No need to start your new plants indoors; this vegetable isn't finicky. Plant the topsets about two inches deep and they'll grow. You can even throw them on the ground to root on their own. The only thing that prevents this unique plant from growing is mucky soil.

GROWING

Walking onions are also called "forever onions" because, once established, they keep growing with little to no help. Topsets form at the tips of the leaves, making the plant bend over and fall. The fallen topsets then root and grow into mature plants the following season. Plants die back and look scruffy over the winter, but each spring they burst forth with new green growth. By late summer, the green stocks can be two feet tall or larger, and topsets will form. They start out tiny and green but grow into larger bulbs and develop reddish-brown skins.

CHALLENGES

The only problem you'll have with walking onions is trying to keep them from spreading all over your garden. Thankfully, they're easy to pull out and even easier to introduce into your dinner recipes. To keep your onions in check, stop the topsets from taking root once they fall over. Add mulch in the fall to protect the shallow bulbs from hard winter freezes.

HARVEST

The entire plant is edible, from the shallot-like roots to the topsets and hollow leaves, so go ahead and harvest every part of this amazing crop. Pick the hollow green leaves as soon as they sprout in the spring; chop them up and eat them like chives or green onions. The topsets are ready to go when the stalk bends over in midsummer. Harvest the shallot roots in late summer, but be aware that they do pack a punch. Make sure to leave a few so new plants will sprout in the spring. Eat them peeled and sautéed (so worth it!), or prepare them just as you would onions or shallots.

TENDER PERENNIALS

PEPPER

While typically grown as annuals, peppers are tender perennials in frost-free places. This means with a little extra care and attention, you can grow them indoors through the winter. Their compact nature makes them perfect for container growing.

Varieties: Peppers can be crisp and sweet or wickedly spicy. Cubanelle peppers are long and thin; they look like they should be hot, but they're not. Italian frying peppers like Jimmy Nardello are best enjoyed gently fried in olive oil, which brings their flavor to a peak. The classic bell pepper tastes great raw. Experiment with different varieties to see which ones you like best.

WHERE IT THRIVES

Regional compatibility: Peppers grow best in southern regions with long, hot summers. In northern climates, it's a race against the clock since peppers tend to ripen in late September. Start seeds or cuttings inside on a heat mat to give peppers a chance to ripen earlier.

Optimal sun and shade: Peppers love the heat of the sun, so plant them where they'll get six to eight hours of it a day.

Resilience: Peppers are heat- and drought-tolerant, making them an excellent choice for sunny, dry gardens. Spicy peppers, in particular, thrive in these conditions and grow hotter because of it. They do not appreciate cold or soggy soil. If peppers get too much water, their leaves wilt away and the fruit drops off.

PLANTING

Best time of year: Start pepper seeds indoors six to eight weeks before your last frost.

Best way to plant: Pepper seeds won't germinate in cold soil, so sow them about one-quarter inch deep in pots or cell flats and keep them warm on a heat mat. When three true leaves appear, transplant the seedlings into larger pots. Move them into your garden after the last frost.

GROWING

Peppers can get a bit top heavy so you might need to support leaning plants with a few bamboo stakes. I make an X with the stakes and place it on the leaning side to keep the plant from tipping over. Since they have shallow roots, peppers will rip right out of the ground if they fall over.

CHALLENGES

Pepper maggots spend their lives inside the fruit after the adult flies lay their eggs. Once hatched, the maggots eat out and rot the insides. They're hard to control but the adults are attracted to the color yellow, so it can help to hang yellow sticky traps in your garden from late May to early June.

HARVEST

All peppers start off green and change color as they ripen. Harvest them right away or wait for the color change for a sweeter pepper. Use scissors to harvest your crop instead of pulling off the peppers by hand. The branches are brittle and easily break away from the plant.

TOMATO

Much like peppers, tomatoes are true perennials but only in frost-free climates. They're also surprisingly drought-tolerant because they grow deep roots that pull moisture from the soil long after the surface has dried out. Heat-loving tomatoes need a long growing season, so plan ahead.

Varieties: Tomatoes come in vining (indeterminant) and bush (determinant) types. Vining types produce lots of fruit that gradually ripen over the season. Determinant types are compact and perfect for containers, but the fruit tends to ripen all at once. Tomatoes come in many varieties: you can choose small and supersweet cherry tomatoes, large and juicy beefsteak tomatoes, or dense and flavorful paste tomatoes.

WHERE IT THRIVES

Regional compatibility: Tomatoes like long, hot summers with lots of sun, but different varieties have adapted to grow just about anywhere. In cooler climates, consider growing early-maturing varieties like Amish Gold.

Optimal sun and shade: Tomatoes need about eight hours a day of direct sunlight to be fruitful.

Resilience: Tomatoes adapt readily to drought conditions once they've matured. In fact, tomatoes grown without much water tend to be higher in nutritional value and more resistant to disease. What affects tomatoes more than water is how hot or cold it is—high heat can cause blossoms to fall off the plant and frost can turn your plants to mush overnight.

PLANTING

Best time of year: Tomatoes need warm weather to grow, so start seedlings inside in the spring about six to eight weeks before the last frost. To plant them outside, you'd have to wait until early summer, which doesn't give the fruit enough time to ripen in northern regions.

Best way to plant: Tomatoes take a long time to grow, so plant indoors up to six weeks before the last spring frost. Push at least two seeds into each cell or pot. When seedlings have two leaves, thin or remove the extra plant, leaving the strongest and healthiest sprout with plenty of room to grow. Tomatoes also like warm soil, so use a heat mat.

GROWING

These plants thrive in containers, especially when sheltered by a protective wall. They can also pump out juicy yet heavy fruits; I once harvested a single tomato that weighed over three pounds! For this reason, the vining variety benefits from support.

Prune your plant back to one or two central stalks and tie each to a sturdy bamboo stake with tomato clips or strips of an old shirt or towel. As the plants grow, they'll push out suckers or new branches where the leaf meets the stem. Remove the suckers so more energy flows into the fruit-bearing central stem, producing bigger, tastier tomatoes.

Determinant types need less attention and can be left to grow as a bushy mess. If the plants get a little top heavy, use bamboo stakes in the form of an X to support them.

CHALLENGES

Tomato hornworms are green caterpillars that can quickly devour tomato leaves. You can try picking them off, but their green color makes them hard to spot. Use an insecticidal soap or Bt to get rid of them. (See "Organic pest solutions," page 134.)

The wireworm, the larval stage of the click beetle, is a silent assassin of newly transplanted tomatoes. The worms sever the stem from the root and damaged plants wither and die before you even realize what's happened. To get rid of them I recommend burying a potato attached to a stick four or five inches deep in your soil. Wireworms love to tunnel into potatoes. After three weeks, dig up your potato trap and remove all the worms you've captured.

HARVEST

Pick tomatoes as they ripen so more of them will grow. They're ready to harvest when they easily pop off the plant from just above the stem. I place my index and middle finger behind the nobbed joint, called the pedicle, and use my thumb to press down, snapping the fruit free. You can also use scissors. In the fall, bring any green fruit inside to protect against the frost. They'll continue to ripen on your counter but won't be as juicy or delicious as vine ripened fruit.

Helping your tender perennials survive winter

You can grow your tender perennials in pots outside during the summer, and move them inside before the first frost to protect their roots. This works well for compact peppers, determinate tomatoes, and tender herbs.

For larger perennials, like vining cherry tomatoes, let the fruit ripen, harvest it, and cut the branches about two inches from the soil before moving the plant inside. The fruit will continue to ripen indoors if it gets enough light. Once you've had your fill of tomatoes, cut back the plant and tuck it away for the winter.

Before bringing them inside, water your plants to reduce the stress of moving. Give them enough that it drains out through the bottom of the pot. Pruning your plants to half their height also helps them survive the transition. Finally, check to see that they're free of bugs and disease so you don't bring in any unwelcome guests.

With the exception of herbs, tender perennials brought inside do not continue to grow. Instead, they sleep, or go dormant. Keep them in a cool but not cold place; around 50 degrees works well for the winter. Water them once a month.

Dormant plants need no sunlight and require little water. As spring approaches, move your plants to a warmer, well-lit area to wake them up. Then watch them grow. Your plants will be hardier and produce food much more quickly than planting from seed.

FAVORITE GARDEN ANNUALS

BEANS

Beans are legumes which means they share a special relationship with rhizobia, bacteria that live within the roots and produce nitrogen compounds that help the plant grow faster. Once a legume dies, nitrogen is released from the roots into the soil for other plants to use. This is why planting legumes like peas and beans is a natural way to fertilize the soil.

Varieties: Beans can grow as a bush or vine. They can be round or flat and range in color from dark purple to green to pale yellow. Some beans, like the Asian long bean, can grow up to two feet in length. Just pick what you'd like to eat.

WHERE THEY THRIVE

Regional compatibility: Beans can grow anywhere in the country. Hot or cold, wet or dry.

Optimal sun and shade: Beans require full sun for more than six hours a day to be productive.

Resilience: Legumes are prolific growers in warm areas but don't do so well in the cold, with a few exceptions. Scarlet runner beans are one example of a bean that can overwinter in some climates. Most beans succumb easily to frost and flooding.

PLANTING

Best time of year: Beans need warm soil (60 to 70 degrees) to sprout, so plant seeds well after the danger of frost has passed.

Best way to plant: It's better to sow seeds directly into the garden rather than start them indoors because bean roots are sensitive to transplantation. Plant seeds two inches apart and roughly one inch deep.

GROWING

Once beans sprout, they're quick to grow. Vining beans do best with the support of a trellis and can grow more than eight feet tall if you let them. Bush beans don't need a trellis but they do need shelter since a strong wind can easily snap their delicate stems. I've planted them between rows of currants, which act as a natural windbreak. You can enjoy beans all summer long if you plant a new batch every three weeks or so.

CHALLENGES

Bean plant leaves are more vulnerable to bugs than their pods. Leafhoppers, tiny, lime-green pests, won't kill plants but can stress them out, making them susceptible to disease and other pests. Signs you may have a hopper problem are curling leaves that yellow at the tips. Shake your vines to see whether adult leafhoppers start hopping about. If you have an infestation, spray the plant periodically with an insecticidal soap.

Mexican bean beetles are also a threat. Look for copper-colored, hard-shelled insects that eat entire leaves, leaving only the veins. Keep them under control by picking off these pesky beetles when you see them. Aphids like to feed on bean leaves too, and while they won't kill your plants, they can transmit a mosaic virus that will. Snip off the affected areas and spray plants with insecticidal soap.

HARVEST

Beans need to be picked constantly to keep the plant productive. Use scissors or your fingernail to snip the pods off your plants, and be careful not to break the delicate vines. To get tender beans, pick them every three to five days.

CABBAGE

Cabbage produces a lot of big outer leaves that can be too tough to eat but will do beautifully in your compost pile. Some varieties grow in the winter, snow and all, even when temperatures dip below 30 degrees.

Varieties: Green and red cabbage are the most popular, and you can eat them fresh or cooked. Tropicana cabbage will grow to a huge size—I use the heads to make giant heaps of slaw. Napa cabbage is tender and the stalks much thinner, making it easy to eat right out of the garden. Savoy cabbage's crinkly, dark green leaves are thick and cold hardy. It's better eaten cooked than raw but either way, it's delicious.

WHERE IT THRIVES

Regional compatibility: Cabbage prefers the cool temperatures of northern climates, but it also grows well in the cooler winters of southern climates.

Optimal sun and shade: While cabbage is a cool-season crop, it loves to bask in the sun. When grown in the shade, the plant produces loose and floppy heads. An afternoon break from the sun can prevent it from bolting or going to seed.

Resilience: Cabbage does very well in the cold.

PLANTING

Best time of year: Because cabbage likes cool weather, spring planting is the best option. If you want mature cabbage before the first fall frost, sow seeds in the late summer. If you live in a warm southern area, plant in the fall and harvest your heads throughout the winter.

Best way to plant: Cabbage seeds are tiny, so try starting them in pots if you have the space. Don't keep them in the pots for too long;

transplant your baby heads into the garden when they're four weeks old to prevent bolting.

GROWING

When I grew cabbage to sell at the farmstand, I learned that most people don't know what to do with a five-pound head. While I proudly displayed my monster cabbages, people kept asking if I had anything smaller. So I started planting it closer together. The smaller heads sold rapidly, proof that not everyone loves cabbage as much as I do.

Be aware that some varieties of cabbage split open after a heavy rain is followed by a dry spell. If this weather pattern is typical where you live, you can slow growth by gently twisting the plant to break some of the roots, or slicing the outer roots with a hoe or weeding knife.

CHALLENGES

Slugs and cabbage loopers tend to find their way into the center of cabbage heads. Not a big deal unless you're managing a farmstand. While the insects don't do much damage, people do not love bugs crawling onto their kitchen counters. I learned to cut the heads and soak them in a tub of cold water outside before bringing them inside. The cold bath forces bugs out of the cabbage.

You can try to keep bugs away naturally by planting it next to aromatic herbs. Peppermint and rosemary will repel the dreaded cabbage butterfly and prevent it from laying eggs that turn into cabbage loopers. Keep cabbage away from strawberries, which can attract cabbage loopers.

HARVEST

For the tastiest result, harvest cabbage when the heads are still growing. Small heads and cabbage that has been hit by a mild frost will be sweeter than cabbage grown entirely in summer conditions. Pick it by using a sharp knife to cut the whole plant at the base of the stem. Remove and compost the loose side leaves.

CARROT

A carrot has a large taproot that, once pulled from the soil, leaves behind a long tunnel. These tunnels open up the soil so air and water can percolate into it and nourish the various organisms that build soil health. Growing carrots is one nice way to aerate your soil.

Varieties: Orange carrots like Danvers and Nantes are the norm, but you can experiment with a wide range of colors. Try growing Purple Dragon, White Satin, Black Spanish, or Kyoto Red carrots, which have unique flavors as well.

WHERE IT THRIVES

Regional compatibility: Carrots can be grown in any region across North America. They prefer cool weather and, in warmer southern regions, do better if planted in early spring or late fall.

Optimal sun and shade: Carrots prefer at least six to eight hours of sun a day but grow fine in partial shade; they'll just mature more slowly. In shady gardens, you'll have to wait a little longer for your crop.

Resilience: Carrots are relatively drought-tolerant if given plenty of water early on in the growing season. Thirsty roots may crack under too much water stress but will still taste good.

PLANTING

Best time of year: You can plant carrots any time of the year as long as the soil is warm enough to dig in. Carrots are sweetest after they've been hit by a light fall frost.

Best way to plant: Carrots have long, tiny seeds that grow best when you plant them directly in the ground, either in neat rows or scattered around the garden.

GROWING

Carrots grown in dense soil tend to be stunted, twisted, or split. Loose, sandy soil will give you long, straight carrots. The tops of the root that stick out of the soil can get sunburned. You can prevent this by gently pushing soil up around the base of the stem; think of it as sunscreen for your carrots.

CHALLENGES

My early-season crop used to get hit with carrot rust fly almost every year, producing a nearly inedible crop ruined by tunneling baby maggots. I now plant carrots later in the season, after the rust flies have gone.

HARVEST

Harvest carrots at any time. To get them out of the ground, pull the leafy green tops slowly so as not to separate them from the root. If your soil is loose, the carrot will pop out easily. If it's dense, you may need a little extra help from a trowel.

CUCUMBER

This quick-to-mature plant produces an ample harvest, even in regions with short growing seasons. Train cucumbers up a trellis and you can plant heat-sensitive plants like lettuce and spinach in their shade.

Varieties: A surprising number of varieties exist, ranging from vining types to bushes. My personal favorite is the lemon cucumber, which grows as yellow-and-white balls that look beautiful in salads. Certain types of cucumbers include a bitter-tasting chemical that makes them hard to digest. This is why many popular varieties have been bred for thinner skins, fewer seeds, and sweetness.

WHERE IT THRIVES

Regional compatibility: While the plants are quick to mature and produce many tasty cucumbers, they need warm weather to grow and thrive. In southern regions, they benefit from afternoon shade once temperatures soar above 90 degrees. In northern climates, plant them outside only after nighttime temperatures climb above 50 degrees.

Optimal sun and shade: You'll get the biggest harvest if you give cucumbers six to eight hours of sunlight a day. Cucumbers grown in shady spaces don't produce much fruit.

Resilience: As with many annuals, cucumbers are extremely frost sensitive. They don't start growing to their true potential until the soil has warmed to around 70 degrees.

PLANTING

Best time of year: Cucumbers need heat to grow. Plant them in early summer for the best results.

Best way to plant: Get a head start on your cucumber crop by planting the seeds inside three weeks before your last frost. They like bottom heat so a heat mat can be helpful. Once they sprout, remove the heat mat. Cucumbers have relatively sensitive roots and may not do well after being transplanted, so plant them in biodegradable pots. Or just push seeds directly in the ground when it's warm outside, about one inch deep and fifteen inches apart.

GROWING

Cucumbers are fast-growing, vining plants that by season's end can take up a lot of space. If you're short on space, train your plants up by using a trellis, and make sure it's sturdy enough to hold the weight of a bumper harvest. Training your cucumbers will also keep the fruit off the ground and safely away from soil pests. Create a wooden frame in the shape of an upside-down V and tack netting between the supports. Then, gently train the running vines up by weaving them between the pockets of netting.

Cucumbers are about 95 percent water, so they need about one inch of water a week once the fruit begins to ripen. Regular watering also helps the plants develop a healthy root system.

CHALLENGES

Cucumber beetles, striped or spotted beetles about an inch long, will feast on the leaves and stress the plant so it produces only stunted fruit, and not much of it. Plant a few radishes among your cucumber plants to repel the beetles, and let them grow all season without harvesting. Or make a beetle trap by setting out a cup of water mixed with a few drops of neem oil. (See "Organic pest solutions," page 134.)

HARVEST

How you harvest cucumbers depends on what you plan to do with them. If you want to make pickles, harvest when they're small, about three or four inches long. Some cucumbers can grow to over a foot long, while others will mature at six inches. Check the seed packet to see how big your cucumbers are expected to get. If you let them grow too big, they'll be bitter and filled with seeds.

Use a harvesting knife to pick cucumbers so you don't damage the tender vines. Leave a one-inch section of the stem attached to the fruit and it will store longer.

GARLIC

Most gardeners grow garlic as an annual, digging up the heads each summer. But I like to think of garlic as a gateway perennial. If you leave a few heads in the ground over the winter, a new crop will emerge in the spring, all on its own.

Varieties: Garlic comes in two varieties: softneck, which fares better in milder climates; and hardneck, which prefers cooler, northern climates.

WHERE IT THRIVES

Regional compatibility: Most varieties prefer a cool climate; they're resistant to frost, and even a hard freeze, if the soil is well drained. But if you have soggy soil, cold temperatures will freeze the water and pop newly planted cloves right out of the ground, causing them to rot when the soil warms in the spring.

Optimal sun and shade: Garlic grows best in full sun.

Resilience: This plant grows easily and takes up very little space in a garden. As noted above, it's also cold hardy. Visit my garlic bed in late winter and you'll see lots of little green tips poking through the snow.

PLANTING

Best time of year: Garlic is typically planted in the fall a few weeks before the first frost. You can plant it in the spring but the heads will be much smaller. Fall-planted garlic also has a more intense flavor. Make sure to plant it before the ground freezes.

Best way to plant: Break apart the head and plant single cloves in the ground. Depending on the type of garlic, one head can contain as many as 10 cloves. Each clove grows into a full head of garlic.

GROWING

Garlic is cold hardy but still needs protection. I apply a layer of mulch in the fall to help the crop weather the long, cold winter. It grows well in light, sandy soil and needs to be watered frequently during dry spells to promote healthy root development. Once garlic is established, it can tolerate drought.

Garlic's pungent odor can keep away deer and rabbits, along with cabbage worms, spider mites, aphids, carrot rust flies, and Japanese beetles. This makes it a good neighbor to beets, celery, carrots, tomatoes, and cabbage. But the chemicals that make garlic a powerful pest deterrent can also inhibit the growth of peas, beans, and asparagus, so keep it separate from those crops.

CHALLENGES

Knowing when to harvest may be your biggest challenge in growing garlic. Harvest too soon and the heads won't mature. Harvest too late and the bulbs may already have begun to open. In neither case will the heads store well.

HARVEST

Garlic bulbs are ready to harvest when the bottom two leaves turn yellow and wither. This typically occurs in July or August. Expect a later harvest date if you plant in the spring. If you want green garlic, harvest it in the early summer when the stalks are young and tender. Green garlic tends to be less pungent.

To harvest garlic, carefully loosen the soil and dig out the heads, taking care not to tear the papery skin. This thin covering protects garlic from going bad once you store it. You can also harvest the garlic scape once it curls. Scapes appear only once a season, so don't miss out. They're delicious sautéed in oil and salted, or used in pesto. Harvest scapes once they begin to curl and before they get too thick and woody.

KALE

This garden annual can be planted as soon as the soil thaws. And unlike other garden annuals, which grow and die quickly, kale grows well into the late fall, sucking down carbon the whole time. I've gone out in the middle of winter to harvest kale, shoveling aside snow until I can grab a few leaves for a hearty winter stew.

Varieties: Red Russian kale has purple stems and chalky green foliage that looks like overgrown oak leaves. There's also curly kale, which ranges from pale to deep green with ruffled edges, while Lacinato kale has slender dark green and blue leaves. I usually grow one of each variety.

WHERE IT THRIVES

Regional compatibility: Kale grows just about anywhere, though it doesn't like extreme heat. Gardeners who live in the South and Southwest tend to grow it as a winter crop.

Optimal sun and shade: Kale grows best in fully sunny locations but it can tolerate partial shade.

Resilience: This is a hardy vegetable and fairly drought-tolerant. But it does better if you can keep it watered during dry periods.

PLANTING

Best time of year: Plant kale in the spring as soon as the soil is warm enough to dig in. For a winter crop, plant it in the early fall or late summer.

Best way to plant: Kale grows from teeny, tiny seeds. I plant them outside in four-inch pots so I can keep the slugs from devouring them before they can grow. I transplant them after they've grown a few leaves. If you want to give direct seeding a shot, push in your seeds one-eighth inch deep and two feet apart.

GROWING

Kale produces plenty of dark green leaves so you'll only need a few of these robust plants, which is a good thing because they take up a lot of space.

CHALLENGES

Aphids, slugs, and thrips can attack kale and eat the leaves, so check the leaves regularly to pick off pests. If they persist, spray the leaves weekly with a natural pest solution, like an insecticidal soap.

HARVEST

I grow kale all season long, harvesting the lower leaves as needed when the plants grow tall. By the end of the fall, they look like miniature palm trees, with long, straight stalks and tufted green tops.

LETTUCE

Lettuce gets along with just about everything in the garden. This allows you to plant it among your other plants, thereby packing more plants (and roots) into the soil. They grow quickly, so by the time the larger plants need extra room, your salad greens are ready to harvest.

Varieties: You can grow lettuce as a loose-leaf patch or a compact head. Summer crisp types stay sweet despite the heat and are a nice choice for midsummer planting. Butter lettuce forms compact heads. Romaine has a signature crunch, with the prized hearts at the center of each head. Bibb types have a sweet, buttery taste and ruffled outer leaves. Loose-leaf lettuce grows as individual leaves, allowing you to pick exactly what you need rather than harvesting a whole head.

WHERE IT THRIVES

Regional compatibility: Lettuce can grow anywhere but does better in the coolness of spring than in the heat of summer. In hot regions, grow lettuce as a winter crop.

Optimal sun and shade: It grows best in full sun but appreciates shade in midsummer heat.

Resilience: This leafy green doesn't handle dry conditions, heat, or humidity well, but it is a choice crop for cold-weather growing. In all but the coldest regions, lettuce can grow through the winter with a little protection.

PLANTING

Best time of year: You can plant lettuce all year long, but it prefers cooler weather.

Best way to plant: Plant lettuce seeds in pots or directly in the ground. I grow my head-type varieties in pots before transplanting them because bigger plants have a better chance of reaching maturity. Tender, smaller plants are easy prey for garden pests.

If you want a big patch of loose-leaf lettuce, plant seeds directly in the ground and don't bother with transplanting. It's okay to lose a few plants to bugs. The key is getting the right density: too dense and you'll have mold issues. Too spread out and you'll waste space. Aim to plant seeds in patches, spacing seeds every half-inch. Keep the soil surface moist until seeds germinate.

GROWING

I love salad so much I eat it for breakfast, lunch, and dinner in the summer. There's something about the crisp, fresh crunch of freshly picked greens that I want at every meal. To make sure I have lettuce all season long, I stagger my plantings.

Every two weeks or so, I harvest what's ready and plant a new batch in the same space. The only things that interrupt my unending harvest are slugs, caterpillars, beetles, and rabbits—the creatures that love the delicate greens as much as I do. I also worry hotter summers will threaten this cool season crop, in spite of the afternoon shade I give it.

CHALLENGES

Growing lettuce all summer long can be a challenge since heat stress can make your plants taste bitter. One indication your lettuce is ruined is if you cut into it and white juice spurts from the wound. I use shade cloth to give the tender heads a break from the heat, or plant them among my late-season peas.

HARVEST

You can harvest lettuce at any stage of growth. Pick individual leaves or the whole head.

PEAS

Peas are legumes and naturally add nitrogen to the soil. When planted in dense rows, they shade the soil, helping to keep weeds away. In the fall, leaving a few pods on the vine to dry out and crack open ensures your pea patch will come back each spring without having to replant it.

Varieties: If you want a traditional garden pea, choose Early Perfection or Garden Sweet, which have inedible pods and big, juicy peas. If you want a satisfying crunch and much less work, plant snow or sugar snap peas, which can be eaten right off the vine, pod and all. Popular snow-pea varieties are Sugar Daddy and Oregon Sugar Pod; these varieties produce tiny peas wrapped in a flat pod. Snap peas like Sugar Snap and Sugar Ann have inflated round pods with large peas.

WHERE THEY THRIVE

Regional compatibility: Peas have a limited time to grow before the weather gets too hot (or too cold, for fall plantings). In southern regions, plant peas as a winter crop to avoid the heat.

Optimal sun and shade: Peas like at least six hours of sun a day but start to fade when summer heat sets in. Extend your harvest by planting a late crop of peas in a shady area of the garden, but be aware they won't mature as quickly as your first crop.

Resilience: Peas don't fare well in the high heat of summer and tend to rot in too much rain. But when planted in the chill of spring, even if just above freezing, peas thrive.

PLANTING

Best time of year: Plant in the spring, and don't worry about a late frost. If you want more peas, plant a second crop in the fall.

Best way to plant: You can plant peas outside as early as four weeks before your last spring frost, but if it's a soggy spring hold off until the soil dries a little or your peas won't sprout. Push them into the ground at least an inch deep and two inches apart. You can start them inside but, given the early start date, there's no real advantage to doing so.

GROWING

These climbers need a support trellis to keep them off the ground. Drive a stake into the soil on either side of your pea patch. Tie twine to the base of one stake and string it across to the other in a straight horizontal line. Start at the base of the poles and work your way up, stringing the twine every four inches to give the peas something to hold on to.

CHALLENGES

Pea shoots and tendrils are delicate and easy to break. It's also easy to overwater your peas and rot the roots. Once established, mature plants need only about a half inch of water per week. Once the pods start to develop, you can increase the amount of water to an inch a week to help them plump up.

HARVEST

Heavily picked pea plants will produce more peas. Peas are ready to pick once they've filled out the pods. Use scissors to clip off the peas so as not to break the delicate vines.

POTATO

This plant is an annual but you don't have to replant it each season. That's because it's nearly impossible to harvest every tuber that grows in your garden. Those left in the ground reliably overwinter and sprout into new plants the following spring. Cover them with a protective layer of mulch and you can have your own "perennial" potato patch.

Varieties: Potatoes come in more than 200 varieties. The most common is the russet potato, with its familiar rough brown skin and white insides. Yellow potatoes, with golden skin and insides, are also popular. Add color to your dishes by planting red potatoes, purple potatoes, or my favorite, beta carotene-rich sweet potatoes. If you're looking for a creamy potato, go with sweet, mild white potatoes. Fingerling potatoes are oblong in shape, come in many different colors, and offer an exceptionally buttery flavor.

WHERE IT THRIVES

Regional compatibility: Potatoes thrive in cool weather. They can tolerate temperatures upwards of 80 degrees but won't produce as many tubers in hot weather. Plant them as a winter crop in hot regions.

Optimal sun and shade: The leaves and stems of potato plants love full sun, but the tubers underground don't. This plant needs mulch to protect tubers from turning green (and unpalatable) in the sun's rays.

Resilience: Potatoes are amazingly adaptable and almost always grow, even when conditions are less than ideal. They are a choice crop for the rocky, dry, and acidic soil found in New England.

PLANTING

Best time of year: They can be planted in the spring but won't start growing until the soil has warmed to around 45 degrees.

Best way to plant: Potato plants grow from tubers planted deep in the ground. You can buy them from the grocery store and plant them—so easy! I dig a trench at least six inches deep and toss them in, about six to eight inches apart.

GROWING

Keep potato vines well watered during the summer, especially throughout the entire flowering stage. This is when the plants create their tubers, so a steady water supply is crucial for a good crop. Potatoes do well with one or two inches of water per week. Stop watering if the foliage turns yellow and begins to wither. This helps cure the potatoes for harvest so they store better once picked.

CHALLENGES

The starchy flesh of potatoes attracts pests, including wireworm, a larval form of click beetles that feed on tubers. Moles, voles, and mice also love to gnaw on them. I always plant a few sacrificial potatoes with my crop. The hungry pests flock to the tubers, which I mark with sticks. After a few weeks I dig them out, along with the bugs that have found their way inside.

Moles and other large pests are a little trickier to curb. I've had success relocating them after setting up a have-a-heart trap near badly chewed plants.

Fungal and bacterial rot can damage the roots, especially if the tubers are grown in damp soil. Fusarium wilt stunts the vines and creates hard, dark spots on the potatoes. Prevention is the best defense, so plant your tubers in well-drained soil. Make sure never to replant infected tubers or use them for seed because disease can be passed along to the next generation.

HARVEST

Unless you have X-ray vision, it's hard to know when potatoes are ready to harvest. One clue is that the vines start to yellow and fall over. Don't wait too long or the vines will die back completely, making it impossible to tell where the tubers are located. You can dig up baby potatoes throughout the season, but eat them within a week because they don't store well.

Harvest your potatoes by slowly and evenly pulling up the stem. If you apply consistent, slow pressure, most of the spuds will stay attached to the plant. Use a pitchfork to dig up the soil around the plant and find any stragglers, or leave them be so they sprout the following year.

RADISH

Radishes are quick to sprout and easy, anything goes plants. As with carrots, harvested radishes leave pockets of space, making it easier for air and water to enter. Plant them around the garden to loosen the soil.

Varieties: Radishes can taste sweet or spicy and be round or long. Their small size makes them perfect for container growing. Try growing Watermelon, French Breakfast, or Amethyst for a peppery crunch. The large winter types are referred to as daikon radishes; try Alpine for a sweet, mild flavor.

WHERE IT THRIVES

Regional compatibility: Radishes can grow in any region at any time but prefer the cool springs found in temperate climates.

Optimal sun and shade: Radishes that grow too fast get woody and tough. Growing them in afternoon shade will keep them nice and tender.

Resilience: Radishes grow in most types of soil at any time of the year.

PLANTING

Best time of year: Plant seeds in the spring for a fall harvest or in the fall for a winter harvest.

Best way to plant: Radishes are the easiest root crop to grow because they have large seeds and sprout very quickly. Plant them directly in the ground up to a half inch deep and an inch apart. If you lose track of your spacing, thin plants once they sprout to achieve the right spacing. The little radish sprouts are delicious in salads.

GROWING

Radishes are particularly juicy when planted near lettuce. Quick-growing radish seeds also make great row markers for slow-to-grow beets and carrots.

CHALLENGES

If you notice your radish leaves starting to curl, you might have an aphid infestation. Check under the leaves for black, orange, or green aphids. These pests will suck the sugar out of your plants. The cabbage maggot is also a problem. Look for wilted leaves and mushy brown tunnels in your radish crop. If you see evidence of cabbage maggots, treat your radishes with Bt or insecticidal soap. The pesky flea beetle is another pest that can infest your radishes. These bugs are not a problem for mature radishes, but the small, circular bites they take out of leaves can kill younger plants.

HARVEST

Radishes mature quickly. If you wait too long to pick them, they become inedible. Pick them before they get bigger than a golf ball, unless they're sweet daikon. These can grow big without losing taste and texture. Harvest your radishes by grabbing hold of the green tops and pulling.

SPINACH

Most leafy greens like spinach are annuals. You can boost the carbon value of annuals by keeping their roots in the ground after the harvest, and building organic matter in the soil around them.

Varieties: My favorites include a savory spinach called Bloomsdale, which has thick and crinkly succulent leaves. Seaside is a flat-leaved variety that tastes good cooked or fresh. Acadia is semi-savory with crisp, flat leaves that are fairly easy to clean. (For what it's worth, I was named after the Park.)

WHERE IT THRIVES

Regional compatibility: Spinach can grow anywhere in the country. In hot and arid regions, grow it as a winter crop.

Optimal sun and shade: This leafy green prefers full sun but in hot places it needs some shade to thrive.

Resilience: Spinach needs six weeks of cool conditions for a good harvest. If you want spinach in the middle of summer, try growing New Zealand or Malabar spinach, two varieties that can handle the heat. They aren't true spinach plants but taste close enough. In warm, frost-free climates these imitation spinach plants can be grown as perennials.

PLANTING

Best time of year: I adore spinach, so on the farm I squeezed in a few rows wherever I could, in the spring and again in the fall.

Best way to plant: Spinach seeds are best planted directly in the ground. If you have a lot of slugs or other hungry insects in your garden, plant your leafy greens in small pots before setting them outside. Bigger, more mature plants have an easier time surviving gnawing bugs.

GROWING

In cool temperatures, spinach needs very little cultivating. But when the days lengthen and the thermostat rises, spinach bolts and produces a long seed stock. You can stave off bolting by keeping the soil moist and mulched. If the plants do bolt, harvest your spinach immediately, before it gets tough and bitter.

CHALLENGES

Bolting can be a problem, so plant it in the shade of larger plants. If you plant in a container, move it out of the afternoon sun to protect against heat stress.

HARVEST

Pick small spinach leaves with scissors by cutting the stems at the base of the leaves. I like to harvest the outer, older leaves first and then gradually work my way into the center as the leaves mature. That way, the plant keeps growing even as I harvest. If I'm really craving the stuff, I cut the whole plant off at the base, leaving the roots untouched.

SQUASH

Squash, with its long vines and large leaves, can protect the soil from getting scorched and prevent weeds from getting out of control. Many indigenous cultures have long recognized and taken advantage of this by planting what are known as the three sisters: corn, beans, and squash grown side by side. The corn provides a natural trellis for the beans, the beans add nitrogen to the soil, and the squash acts as a living mulch.

Varieties: Summer squash has thin, tender skin and can be long or saucer shaped. I grow Sunburst Patty Pan summer squash because the plant is compact, saving space in my garden; it's even small enough to grow in containers. If you want the more traditional summer squash, which is long and green, select the variety known as Green Machine.

Winter squash is grown for its sweet flesh; the tough exterior keeps it from rotting well into the winter months. My favorites are Burgess Buttercup and Thelma Sanders acorn squash. Most squashes grow enormous, but these tiny gems make perfect single servings.

WHERE IT THRIVES

Regional compatibility: Squash can grow anywhere in the United States. Summer squash is easier to grow than winter squash in regions with a short growing season.

Optimal sun and shade: These sprawling plants like at least eight hours of sun. Give them afternoon shade in hot regions when water is scarce.

Resilience: Squash loves the heat and can be mildly drought-tolerant once established in the garden. The plant's large leaves shrivel in dry weather but quickly recover once watered.

PLANTING

Best time of year: Squash is a fair-weather plant that won't do well unless it's planted in the heat of summer.

Best way to plant: Plant squash directly in the ground. These plants have sensitive root structures that don't like to be disturbed. If you start squash indoors, be sure to transplant it before it becomes rootbound.

GROWING

Squash's natural tendency is to sprawl. If you have a small garden, train the vines by pushing a few stakes into the ground about two feet apart and weaving the vines between them. Or just cut back on any unwanted vines. You won't get as much squash that way, but less can be best with this fast-growing vegetable.

CHALLENGES

A wide range of rots, wilts, and blights can weaken or kill squash during the summer. Fortunately, this happens late enough in the season that the plants are well established and don't need the leaves that might wither away. To help prevent fungal disease, water only the base of the plant, not the leaves.

HARVEST

Summer squash left on the vine too long will get pulpy and seedy, so pick it when it's younger and more tender. Check your plants daily once they start to produce, and snip them off the vine with scissors.

Winter squash is different. Leave it on the vine until the end of the season. You can pick it, and clear away the vines, at the same time. Cut the vines at the base of the stem so you can leave the roots in the soil. Winter squash stores well in a cool dark place.

Regenerative gardening calls for a shift in mind-set. Instead of considering our yard an extension of self or ego, we can think about it as a biological system, valuable in its own right, over which we have stewardship.

We are privileged to have an impact on the little ecosystem that contains our home, and the way we do that says a lot about our values. Do we use poison? Do we monocrop and cover our entire yard with lawn? How fixated are we on maximizing, or even just obtaining, a yield? What roles do values such as recreation, beauty, utility, convenience, and diversity play in how we treat our land?

The regenerative garden is for people who see a garden or yard, at least in part, as an opportunity to heal our relationship with the Earth, and grow a bunch of healthy food in the process. Part of that healing may involve relinquishing a little control for the greater good. Cultivating biological diversity in our yards and gardens, for instance, could help us hone our own stewardship practices.

It could work like this: maybe your neighbor has a beautiful, prolific plum tree. You might think, "Ah, plum trees grow well here—I'll find out what kind it is and buy one myself!" A more regenerative approach, however, would be to think about another plant that might benefit your community. If you were to plant an apricot or a fig tree instead, you would introduce greater diversity into the ecosystem of your yards—and maybe trade your surplus figs for the neighbor's extra plums.

—Michael Weaver
Chelsea Green Publishing

KEEP IT GOING

Before summer begins to thrum with all the weeding, planting, and pest swatting that is part of growing food, I like to stand in my garden. For me, few places are more appealing than a plot filled with tender green shoots. It's all promise, no work, and it energizes me with its suggestion of what's to come. This is also my chance to inhale the sweet smell of healthy soil. That scent you're hit with after fresh rain falls on warm soil. The reason certain root vegetables, like beets and carrots, taste earthy. The reassuring stench released by *Streptomyces* bacteria when they die.

Fragrant soil indicates the presence of other bacteria as well, along with fungi and insects that aid in plant growth. When I scoop up a handful of earth, I look for crumbly soil threaded through with mycelium fibers and enough air pockets that it resembles a sponge. These pockets enable soil to hold on to nutrients and water through dry and difficult times, and make great homes for the worms and other hardworking soil organisms helping to build carbon-rich soil.

Each growing season is another chance to feed these hungry soil organisms, layer on more organic matter, and deepen the carbon sink under your feet.

SPRING: Feed the soil

Root out weeds while they're small. Before spreading the season's first layer of compost or mulch, invest some time in thoroughly weeding your garden beds. Do it when the weeds are still tender and easier to pull out. The mulch you'll add later on will discourage new weed growth, but it won't do much to kill off the ones that are already well established, so keep at it. After a few seasons of aggressive weeding, there won't be any left to pull.

Prune your plants. Trim away dead, diseased, or broken branches from plants that have lived through the winter. Since pruning stimulates plant growth, spring is the best time to do it. (If you prune in the fall, right before the cold, any new growth will likely freeze and die, wasting valuable energy that could have gone towards enduring the harsh winter months.)

Always snip to a leaf bud, the place where the leaf grows from. You'll recognize it as little bumps on a plant stem. Try to cut as close to a bud as possible, otherwise you'll leave a stub of the stem above the bud that could rot and harm your plant.

Feed the soil with compost. Each spring you'll want to replenish any nutrients that have been lost over the winter with a big dose of fresh compost. Mix at least one inch of compost into the first few inches of soil and spread it with a rake before planting. If your perennials are well established, just add it to the base of your perennials. No need to mix it in.

After you add the compost, it's time to aerate, or loosen, the soil to create a welcoming bed for your seeds and transplants. The gentlest, most effective way to break up the soil is with a broadfork, a heavy U with metal tines (see page 65). But a pitchfork is fine, too.

Boost with extra fertilizer as needed. In the early spring, I sometimes add a nitrogen-heavy fertilizer to help my plants really take off.

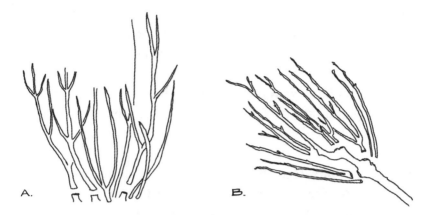

A) Cut away diseased branches or stems from your perennials by snipping them at the base. B) If you want to control the size of your tree or shrub, avoid making too many smaller cuts. Instead, cut roughly two thirds of a branch back to a leaf node, or bud.

You don't need much. Overfertilizing can produce spindly plants, and regular dosing with compost and mulch is often enough.

Add mulch. Give your plants, old and new, a layer of mulch to check the growth of the summer weeds to come. First, sprinkle the ground with water. Then scoop mounds of mulch onto your garden bed every few feet, using a rake to smooth the piles. You want an even layer at least one inch thick, but the deeper the mulch, the better it works. I push any excess material a couple of inches away from the base of my plants to prevent stems from suffocating and rotting. For larger plants and trees, I keep mulch at least eight inches from the base. If you're still having trouble with weeds later on, or your soil is quick to dry out, add some more.

SUMMER: Tend to your garden

Weed, weed, weed. Weeds will always be a problem, and as the climate changes you'll have to be alert to new invasives moving further north. Even if you rid your whole neighborhood of weeds, birds will still drop seeds from above. But weed for a few seasons and most will eventually go away. One tip: clear, mow, or weed-whack the perimeter of your garden to help block the arrival of new weeds.

Continue building your compost pile. All summer long, I stockpile grass clippings, garden debris, and leaves in my compost pile. I use so much it's helpful to have a ready supply.

Add more plants. If you had a busy spring and missed your window to plant your favorite foods from seed, don't worry—you still have time to pop plants in the ground if you buy seedlings. Plant, water, and mulch, and you're done. Feel free to add compost to the planting hole as well. But if you've been nourishing your soil with it regularly, don't bother—your soil is rich enough to support your new plants. You can ease heat stress for your new plants by moving them into the ground early in the morning, late in the evening, or on a cloudy or rainy day.

Support your plants. Some perennials and annuals like a little support, whether from a trellis or stake. I've used sticks and old T-shirts, or shoelaces, in a pinch. By preventing plants from flopping over, you keep them off the ground so they're less likely to be trampled on, gobbled up, or uprooted.

Water your plants, but not too much. Established perennials more or less fend for themselves, finding pockets of water stashed away from the last rainstorm. But annuals like a steady supply. Also, with all the freaky weather that's happening, who knows when your region will be hit by a record-breaking drought?

So I rely on drip irrigation, a series of inexpensive plastic tubes that trickle water. It's better than using a hose or sprinkler because it uses water efficiently, dripping it right into the root zone. I was able to cut my farm's total water bill by a third by installing one. It also prevents overwatering.

If you're not planning on installing an irrigation system, you can avoid overwatering by regularly sticking a finger into the soil. If it feels dry at the tip, it's time to water. If it's still moist, hold off. For young plants, which need more moisture, water them when the first inch of the soil is dry.

Prune diseased branches or stems. Summer pruning isn't all that necessary, unless you have diseased branches or need to whack back a plant that's growing too big. As a general rule, I never remove more than a third of the plant at once. The same goes for harvesting.

One common mistake gardeners make when trying to control the size of their plants is called stubbing out. This happens when you cut the same branch or stem over and over again. Since pruning stimulates growth, the cut stub responds by sprouting many new branches. The more you snip, the more new tips you get—and have to snip again. Avoid this by making fewer, larger cuts (see page 131).

Boost with extra fertilizer as needed. So much energy goes into ripening food that sometimes plants get stressed and emit distress signals that attract pests. If you notice your plants struggling, consider giving them a dose of potassium to prevent stress, or phosphorus to help fruit ripen faster.

Fend off pests. Bugs are worse than weeds, which says a lot, and summer brings a lot of them. Take a lap around your garden every week to hunt for unwanted bugs by scanning for dead zones, wilted or discolored leaves, and unusual growth or lack of fruit. When I see an unhealthy plant, I gently turn over the leaves to look for the culprit. See five aphids on your currants? Brush them off; problem solved.

You can be proactive and keep the bugs off your plants with row covers, or lightweight pieces of fabric, draped over your plants. Remember to remove the fabric periodically while your plants bloom so pollinators can find them.

ORGANIC PEST SOLUTIONS

The first step to controlling pests using organic solutions is to know how to find them.

Type of pest	Name	What they look like
Suckers	Aphid	Minute, pear-shaped bugs that range in color from red, yellow, green, and black. These messy eaters leave sugary, sticky drippings all over plants. The sugary residue grows sooty mold, which looks like somebody smeared wood ash all over your gorgeous plants.
	Leafhopper	More than 20,000 different kinds of leafhoppers are sucking the life from plants all over the world. A common type is the potato leafhopper, which is lime green and moves sideways.
	Thrips	Young thrips are tiny lime-green bugs with feathery wings to the side. Adult thrips turn a dark brown or black and grow only as thick as a sewing needle.
	White flies	Tiny moth-like bugs with powdery white wings. Usually attack in large numbers.
	Scale	These weird bugs are immobile and look like small, legless oval bumps. Their look is due to a protective covering they secrete to stave off predators while feeding.
	Spider mites	Miniature ticks.
Defoliators	Caterpillar	The larval stage of flying insects like moths and flies. Cabbage loopers can eat up to three times their own body weight.
	Beetles	More than 12,000 kinds of beetles live in the United States. The hard shell acts as a coat of armor. Infestations can destroy so many leaves your plants won't be able to photosynthesize.
	Slugs and snails	A soft and smooth body that is actually a single muscle. Each leaves a tell-tale trail of slime in their wake.

Where you'll find them	What to do
On the stems of new growth or under leaves.	Spray with insecticidal soap, or hose off bugs with water.
On the underside of leaves. Search for them by gently shaking your plant to see if they leap off in surprise. A trademark of leafhopper feeding is yellowish, dappled leaves that curl up and turn grey or black.	Drape plants with floating row covers, sprinkle on diatomaceous earth (DE), or spray on insecticidal soap.
On tender parts of the plant, such as buds, flowers, and new leaves.	Spray with neem oil or insecticidal soap and/or catch them with sticky traps.
Gathered at the tops of plants or near the ends of stems. If you can't see them, try shaking the plants and watch for a cloud of white flies.	Catch with yellow sticky traps, or spray with neem or horticultural oils.
Twigs, leaves, branches, and fruit.	Spray with neem oil or insecticidal soap.
On the underside of leaves. They are so small you'll need a hand lens to spot the colonies. You can also look for very fine webbing left behind.	Spray bugs with neem oil or insecticidal soap, and keep dust on plants to a minimum.
On the underside of leaves or on plant stems. Some build shelter, meticulously folding or rolling leaf edges around them for protection, which makes them harder to spot.	Remove the caterpillars by hand and place them in a lidded bucket or jar. Or use row covers to keep them off plants. You can also spray them with Bacillus thuringiensis (Bt).
On plants and in the air and soil around plants.	Use row covers, insecticidal soap, garlic-pepper spray, or neem oil. Or remove by hand. Hang colorful sticky traps.
Cool, damp, and shady areas, particularly at night or early morning.	Spread iron phosphate slug bait or diatomaceous earth (DE). Or trap them by laying down pieces of plywood during the heat of day. After a few hours, lift the boards and toss the bugs, or walk them across a street; sun-baked asphalt is a barrier they won't want to cross.

Chart continues on next page

PESTS (*continued*)

Type of pest	Name	What they look like
Soil dwellers	Cutworms	A soft-bodied, grey, yellow or dark brown caterpillar. They curl up when disturbed.
	Wireworm	Tough and shiny yellow skinned worms with three pairs of legs just behind the head.
Animals	Deer, rabbits, birds, moles, voles, chipmunks, raccoons	Think pests with big teeth!

KEY TO ORGANIC PEST SOLUTIONS

BACILLUS THURINGIENIS (Bt): Bt is a naturally-occurring bacteria that ruptures the internal organs of leaf-eating insects like caterpillars. It only works on the bugs that eat treated leaves. It has no impact on pests that are directly sprayed so bees and other pollinators won't suffer.

DIATOMACEOUS EARTH (DE): DE is made from the pulverized fossils of tiny sea creatures and looks like broken glass if you peer at it under a microscope. It kills insects by slicing up their protective outer layer and causes fatal dehydration when they walk through the dusty white powder. You can dust the leaves of your plants to kill leaf-eating bugs or create a barrier of white powder at the base of your plants to stop slugs.

INSECTICIDAL SOAPS: Insecticidal soaps are an effective way to control soft-bodied insects if no beneficial bugs are around to do the job for you. The fatty acids in insecticidal soaps break down the protective cuticles of soft-bodied pests like aphids and caterpillars, which become dehydrated and die. Soap sprays only kill insects that are sprayed directly so be sure to thoroughly wet both sides of leaves and avoid spraying beneficial insects, like wasps and spiders. Repeat applications every five to seven days, as new pests hatch and form colonies.

Or bring in a few birds. Chickens and ducks happily hunt down pests, like wood bugs and slugs, and gobble them up. If you're not up for the work involved in maintaining a flock of domestic birds, invite wild ones over by putting up nesting boxes for them to sit in. I sprinkle seeds and dried flowers around the garden all year long so birds have a reason to stick around.

Where you'll find them	What to do
On plant stems at night and in the soil during the day. Affected roots have galls or lesions, excessive branching, or injured tips.	Spray plants with Bacillus thuringiensis (Bt) or spread on Diatomaceous earth (DE).
Underground, generally in grassy areas. They attack roots, stems, tubers, and bulbs. Weakened plants yellow, wilt, and become stunted or die.	Place a protective ring of Diatomaceous Earth (DE) around young plants. Or use the potato trap method on page 119.
In gardens, rubbing against trees, topping off bushes.	Spray plants with essential oils, Plantskydd, or predator urine. Hang fake predators like owls or falcons. Use flash tape on fences or motion-sensored sprinklers and lights to scare them at night. Build a fence or catch them in no kill traps.

NEEM OIL: Using neem oil is a great preventive control measure. It comes from the bark and leaves of the Neem tree, a common evergreen grown in tropical and subtropical regions. Azadirachtin, the active ingredient in neem oil, makes insects grow slowly and eat less. It also makes them lose interest in laying eggs so there are fewer of them to begin with. Neem is particularly effective against fast growing beetles, small caterpillars, and aphids. Use neem on plants as soon as you see the first adult bug, and spray weekly. Keep your bees safe by covering treated plants with a row cover.

PLANTSKYDD: Plantskydd is environmentally safe and works against rabbits, voles, moose, chipmunks, squirrels, nutria, beaver, groundhogs, and deer. It can last up to six months—even over the winter season. It repels, according to company literature, by "emitting an odor that browsing animals associate with predator activity, stimulating a fear-based response that will have garden feeders looking for somewhere else to dine."

Your goal should never be to have a bug-free garden. You need spiders to eat flies, mosquitoes, beetles, and other insects. Dragonflies, which feed on other flying insects, particularly midges and mosquitoes. And pollinators, which include various types of bees, pollen wasps, butterflies, and moths. You don't want to use pesticides that would harm them. Also, what's wrong with eating greens with a few holes in them? If you do decide to use sprays, select organic controls to minimize the negative side effects.

FALL: Prepare for winter

Rearrange and divide. Fall is a good time to divide up the perennials that are getting crowded, and spread them around. Creating enough space for plants to grow helps keep them healthy, plus it's an easy (and cheap!) way to expand your garden. Work a shovel around the margins of the plant, pushing up and down on the handle to wiggle it loose. When the plant is freed, drive the shovel into its center and break it in two. Plant the new chunk in a new spot, and the parent plant will be happier for the extra space.

Fall is also a good time to plant new perennials. Aim to do it ahead of the first frost so they have time to grow roots before winter arrives.

Add your second dose of compost. Cover your soil with up to an inch of compost to give all those good soil organisms a chance to multiply come spring. If you don't have enough, or your pile isn't ready yet, throw on a little extra compost in the spring.

Leave roots in the ground. After harvesting, cut your annuals off at the base, leaving the roots. The leftover roots help anchor the soil, preventing the wind and rain from washing it away. (Occasionally, an annual will survive the winter—like the spinach in my cold zone 6a garden that regrew this spring.)

Cleaning up the above ground growth of your annuals is important because it helps curb disease. As for my perennials, unless they're sick, I rarely cut them back. I tidy up in the spring by snipping back the previous year's growth, but nothing extreme.

If you have fruit trees or berry bushes, clean up all the fallen fruit. Disease and pests can live on in the mush, reemerging to wreak havoc the following spring.

Protect your plants with mulch. Now's the time to shore up your garden against frost. When soil is exposed to the cold, roots can die, along with beloved soil organisms. Mulching gives them a warm, safe home to hunker down in. Perennials appreciate the cover, which protects them from increasingly frequent temperature fluctuations. It can also help keep compost from being washed away.

I mulch plants with straw piled at least two inches over the base of the plant to help them through the winter. In the spring, I pull most of it away but leave a ring around plant stems to help the soil warm up more quickly. Shredded dry leaves, hay, and wood chips make other fine mulching options.

Water your fall garden. It's easy to forget about watering your plants when the weather starts cooling, but roots tend to grow well now and if your perennials experience a dry fall, they'll suffer. That said, water requirements aren't as intense in the fall as they are in summer. Give your garden a good soak with a hose every week or two, if there's no rain.

Bring tender plants inside. Tomatoes and peppers are examples of tender perennials—plants that cannot survive a light frost and must be brought inside during the winter. While they won't grow much if at all during the winter, they are rooted and ready to go come spring. Plus you get the chance to eat home-grown tomatoes and peppers in December.

Seasonal checklist

Spring: Feed the soil

- ☑ Root out weeds while they're new and easy to pull up.
- ☑ Prune your plants.
- ☑ Feed the soil with compost.
- ☑ Sow new plants.
- ☑ Boost with extra fertilizer, as needed.
- ☑ Add mulch.

Summer: Tend your garden

- ☑ Weed, weed, weed.
- ☑ Continue building your compost pile.
- ☑ Add new seedlings.
- ☑ Support climbing plants with ties or trellises.
- ☑ Water your plants, but not too much.
- ☑ Prune back extra growth.
- ☑ Boost with extra fertilizer, as needed.
- ☑ Fend off pests.

Fall: Prepare for winter

- ☑ Rearrange and divide.
- ☑ Add your second dose of compost.
- ☑ Leave roots in the ground.
- ☑ Protect your plants with mulch.
- ☑ Water the garden.
- ☑ Bring tender plants inside.

QUESTIONS

Do I need to use fertilizer in addition to compost?

I tend not to use anything other than compost to keep my soil healthy, and if you dose your soil once or twice a year with it, along with mulch, you probably won't either. But soil can become exhausted if you've been growing in the same spot for years, or rely on planters or raised beds.

One way to find out whether your soil needs a boost is to get a soil test. Since a basic test reports a fraction of the nutrients available to plants, I recommend acting on it only if you get a really low number for potassium, nitrogen, or phosphorus. Keep in mind there's a thin line between fertilizing and overfertilizing your food crops. Since I favor perennials, which are low maintenance anyway, my particular challenge is making sure I don't overdo it. Too much, and my plants can suffer.

For new gardeners, I've put together a list of organic fertilizers. They supply the basics that plants need to grow. Nitrogen is a nutrient that helps plants photosynthesize and make food for themselves. It also helps build cell walls so plants can grow. Potassium prevents plants from wilting and controls how juicy your tomatoes will be and how succulent your cucumbers. It also helps plants deal with stress from pests, drought, and overfertilization. And phosphorus helps plants develop healthy roots, stems, and branches, as well as grow more flowers and fruits.

Look for the Organic Materials Review Institute (OMRI) certification on any fertilizers you buy. OMRI is an international nonprofit that decides which products meet its stringent standards for "organic."

To use fertilizer, mix it into the first three inches of your soil before planting and once more midway through the growing season. For established plants, add a little to the base. Any of the following can be used as a stand-alone soil conditioner.

Good all-purpose fertilizers

Homemade compost: Store-bought fertilizers are expensive, but making your own compost is always free. In fact, if you have to pay to get your trash hauled away, composting can save you money by reducing the amount of waste you toss. (See "Compost materials," on page 46, for tips on how to create fertilizer from food and yard waste.)

Mycorrhizal inoculant: Mycorrhizal fungi (my-cor-rye-zal) are a group of fungi that form valuable relationships with plant roots. A network of mycelium, or long white strings akin to fungal roots, attaches to plant roots and dramatically increases a plant's ability to absorb nutrients and water. This isn't a true fertilizer because it has no nutritional content, but it helps plants get more out of the soil. I mix it into my compost and mulch piles so that when I spread them in the spring, I inoculate my whole garden.

Fish emulsion: Fish emulsion is a liquid fertilizer made from by-products of the fishing industry. I use this well-balanced and fast-acting fertilizer all season long on my heavy feeders. It does have a very fishy smell, but a few drops of lavender oil can help to mask the odor.

Particularly good for jump-starting spring growth

Manure compost: Manure from herbivores and poultry is a great source of nitrogen and organic matter and generally packs more punch than homemade compost. I get mine from a nearby farm, but you can also just buy ready-made composted manure from your local garden store. Compost manure for at least three months to kill weed seeds and diseases before adding it to a garden. If that's not possible, you can minimize the risk of weeds by using manure from chickens instead of from horses or cows. If you have your own chickens, simply compost the manure with bed material like wood shavings or sawdust. The combination of green manure with brown bed material produces the perfect ratio of nitrogen to carbon for composting.

Blood meal: A dry powder made from cow blood, blood meal is a fast-acting source of nitrogen. I use it in soils with a serious lack of nitrogen to fire up spring growth. Adding too much will make your soil acidic, so always test your soil. If I'm looking to boost nitrogen midseason, I use a plant-based alternative like alfalfa meal, which is gentle and supplies other beneficial nutrients that help feed soil microbes.

Particularly good for maximizing production

Bone meal: Made from ground-up animal bones, bone meal is widely used to replenish phosphorus and calcium. I like to mix bone meal with composted manure for a potent all-around fertilizer for spring. In the fall, when I plant flower bulbs and garlic, I add bone meal to the bottoms of the holes to promote fall root growth before the winter freeze. Since phosphorus-rich fertilizers like bone meal are particularly important for new plants, I sometimes add it directly to the soil when I'm transplanting seedlings to get them off to a good start.

Greensand: This popular fertilizer is collected from the ocean floor and a good source of iron, potassium, magnesium, and dozens of other trace minerals. Greensand breaks up clay soils and makes it easier for sandy soils to retain water. It's very gentle, which means you can't add too much. You can even use it around seedlings and sensitive plants.

Guano: The droppings of seabirds and bats, guano has been harvested from coastal cliffs and dry caves for hundreds of years. Not only does it add nutrients, it's full of microbes that help deter parasitic soil creatures like nematodes. You can buy it as an odorless powder.

Particularly good for fighting pests and climate stress

Kelp meal: Kelp meal is made from dried ocean seaweed and full of nutrients, especially potassium. You can buy a bag of it or get permission to collect it from your local beach. An exceptionally renewable source of potassium,

COMMON DISEASES AND ORGANIC CONTROLS

Gardeners can fend off and treat plant disease with a variety of organic options. The most common course of action is to spray a treatment directly on the infected leaves, or mix it into a bucket of water per the label instructions and pour the solution on the soil around your plants.

Disease	What it attacks
Anthracnose	Tomatoes, cucumbers, melons, and beans.
Bacterial leaf spot	Bell peppers, tomatoes, eggplant, white potatoes, stone fruits, and plants belonging to the cabbage family.
Club root	Most plants in the cabbage family.
Downy mildew	All plants are susceptible.
Early blight	Nightshade vegetables, which include tomatoes, white potatoes, eggplants, and bell peppers.
Mosaic virus	Beans, nightshade vegetables, and squash, pumpkins, and gourds.
Powdery mildew	Many fruits and vegetables are susceptible.
Rusts	A wide range of fruits and vegetables, from beans and onions to apples and pears.
Wilt	Many different fruits and vegetables.

the plant grows up to three feet per day in ideal climates. I use kelp meal to treat tired soils that have been intensely cultivated and spray it on my plants to help them resist heat stress and pests.

My plants seem prone to disease. How do I save them?

Dealing with disease can be the most frustrating aspect of growing food. It really pains me to watch a plant wilt just before harvest because it was hit by late-season mildew. To help combat disease, give

What it looks like	How to stop it
Sunken spots with pink centers on fruits and pods	Spray plants with products containing Bacillus subtilis or soluble sulfur.
Dark, wet spots appear on leaves. The spots dry out and leave behind holes.	Spray infected plants weekly with soluble sulfur.
Older leaves turn yellow and drop. Roots appear swollen.	No good organic controls exist for this disease. Consider solarizing the soil to kill the bacteria.
Appears as a whitish fuzz on the bottom of leaves and stems. Older infected leaves develop patches of yellow that turn crisp and brown.	There aren't many effective controls for downy mildew, but you can try spraying infected plants with neem oil or a systemic broad spectrum fungicide with copper.
Brown and black spots appear on leaves, become enlarged and end up looking like ringed bullseyes. Leaves eventually fall off.	Spray diseased plants with products containing Bacillus subtilis or soluble sulfur
Leaves curl or wrinkle and yellow around the veins. Plant growth is stunted.	This is a virus so fungal treatments will not work. Cut down on the number of leafhoppers and aphids, which carry the disease, by spraying leaves with insecticidal soap.
A white dusty cloud of fungal growth on the tops of leaves.	Spray mildewed areas with neem oil.
Orange rings with black centers appear on the tops of leaves.	Spray affected plants with products containing Bacillus subtilis or soluble sulfur.
Plant foliage turns yellow and wilts away.	Use products containing the natural bacteria *streptomyces griseoviridis*, which can be applied as a soil drench or spray.

your plants space. When plants are crowded, they become stressed, stunted, and susceptible to disease. Water your soil, not the leaves or stems, to avoid getting them wet. Wet and soggy conditions promote fungal diseases like powdery mildew.

Never leave infected plants to rot in your garden or add them to your compost pile; there's a good chance your compost won't get hot enough to kill the pathogens responsible. Prune any damaged branches or stems to stimulate fresh new growth and promote better air circulation so disease doesn't spread.

If after all that your plants still develop problems, consider safe and organic ways to manage the disease before it gets out of hand, like using recommended oils, soaps, and antifungal solutions. (See "Common diseases and organic controls," page 144.)

My soil is too acidic or too basic. How do I balance it?

Once again, the best treatment is a heavy dose of organic matter, but some soil needs an extra push. Here in New Hampshire, land of wild blueberries, the soil is naturally very acidic so I lay down lime regularly to neutralize the soil.

Garden soil is sometimes referred to as sour (acidic) or sweet (alkaline). How sweet and sour is indicated by its pH value. The pH scale ranges from 0 (acidic) to 14 (basic), and most plants prefer a neutral medium between 6 and 7. If you're not sure whether you have sweet or sour soil, you can refer back to your soil test or use a home acidity kit.

The pH of soil matters because it has a big influence on how your plants grow and absorb nutrients. If soil is too acidic, plants aren't getting enough vital nutrients like calcium and phosphorus. It can also make iron, aluminium, and lead more soluble, which in large doses can poison you and your plants. In basic soil, plants are missing out on iron, manganese, and phosphorus.

You can add amendments, like elemental or granular sulfur, to make your soil more acidic. If you need to raise the pH, try adding lime. Follow the labeled instructions to make sure you add the right amount because different products have different potencies.

Adjust the pH early in the spring, about a month before planting, because it takes time for lime or sulfur to activate. Test your pH balance regularly. Treating your soil once does not permanently fix the problem; it's something you'll have to include in your annual maintenance routine.

TOOLS FOR BACKYARD CARBON FARMERS

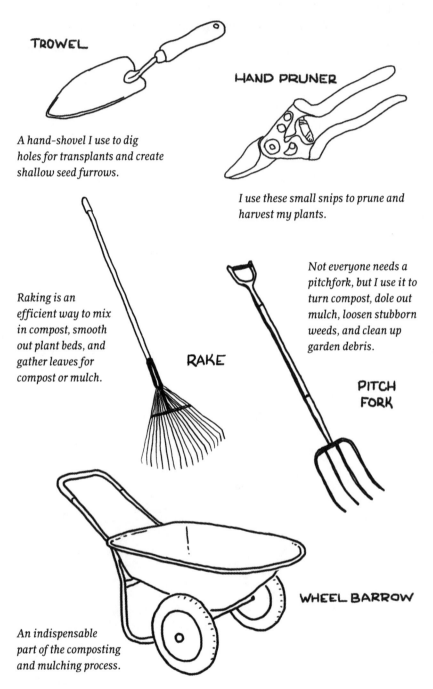

TROWEL

A hand-shovel I use to dig holes for transplants and create shallow seed furrows.

HAND PRUNER

I use these small snips to prune and harvest my plants.

Raking is an efficient way to mix in compost, smooth out plant beds, and gather leaves for compost or mulch.

RAKE

Not everyone needs a pitchfork, but I use it to turn compost, dole out mulch, loosen stubborn weeds, and clean up garden debris.

PITCH FORK

WHEEL BARROW

An indispensable part of the composting and mulching process.

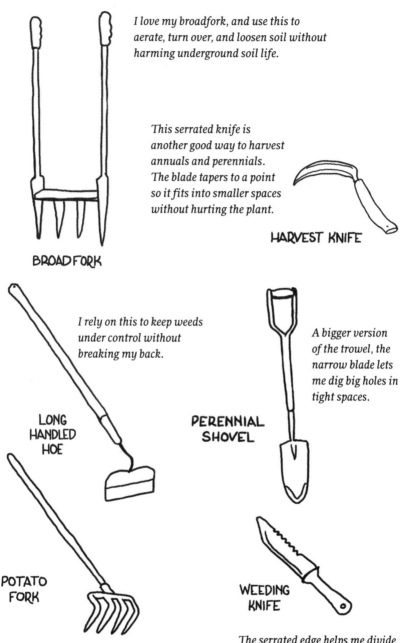

I love my broadfork, and use this to aerate, turn over, and loosen soil without harming underground soil life.

This serrated knife is another good way to harvest annuals and perennials. The blade tapers to a point so it fits into smaller spaces without hurting the plant.

HARVEST KNIFE

BROADFORK

I rely on this to keep weeds under control without breaking my back.

A bigger version of the trowel, the narrow blade lets me dig big holes in tight spaces.

LONG HANDLED HOE

PERENNIAL SHOVEL

POTATO FORK

WEEDING KNIFE

An all purpose tool I use to root out weeds, mix in compost, spread mulch or compost, and shape garden beds.

The serrated edge helps me divide small perennials and dig out stubborn weeds, especially ones with a single taproot.

ACKNOWLEDGMENTS

The chance to turn my passion for growing good food into a book has been a gift. It has given me a way to address the many questions I've been asked as a gardener and farmer. It has forced me to be more thoughtful about how to share that information. And describing the power of regenerative growing has helped me sleep at night when my mind races with all the what-ifs brought on by fears of global warming.

This book could not have been produced without the help of many good people. Monica Stanton diligently parsed, fact-checked, and created a narative for the climate regional snapshots. Tia Schwab produced a number of the charts. Abrah Griggs made the book come to life with her thoughtful typesetting and design. Virginia Aronson jumped in to review the book exactly when we needed her.

Illustrator Joe Wirtheim added warmth and style with his illustrations inspired by the World War II Victory garden posters of the 1940s. I can't think of a better representation of artwork for this book. I am honored and humbled to have worked with Clare Ellis. I couldn't have succeeded without her patience, guidance, and expert advice. She gave the book structure and combed through each chapter, many times over, to improve on my work.

To the people of Point Roberts, Washington, thank you for loving my crooked carrots and oversized cabbages. Your support and enthusiasm for good food allowed me to follow my dreams. Thank you, too, to my friends and family who endured two years of canceled plans, missed vacations, and endless excuses about being too busy to socialize. Finally, to Nimbus, my loyal farm dog. Thank you for patrolling the garden and scaring away the bunnies, woodchucks, and deer, well, most of them anyway.

NOTES

CITIZEN GARDENERS UNITE

Our natural landscapes absorb 29 percent of all carbon dioxide emissions. From *Climate Change and Land: an Intergovernmental Panel on Climate Change (IPCC) special report on climate change, desertification, land degradation, sustainable land management, food security, and greenhouse gas fluxes in terrestrial ecosystems* presented its 50th Session held on 2–7 August 2019. The approved Summary for Policymakers (SPM) was presented at a press conference on 8 August 2019. The IPCC is an independent body founded under the auspices of the World Meteorological Organization (WMO) and the United Nations Environment Programme (UNEP).

Global croplands have the potential to store an additional 1.85 gigatons of carbon each year. Soils can act as both a source and sink of carbon depending on how we manage them. The global soil carbon pool, in this study, is measured at one-meter deep and is estimated to hold 2,500 gigatonnes of carbon. Research has shown that how we treat the land can increase soil carbon stocks in agricultural soils with practices like adding compost, cover cropping, mulching, reduced tillage, fertility management, agroforestry, and rotational grazing. Zomer, Robert J., et al. "Global Sequestration Potential of Increased Organic Carbon in Cropland Soils." *Nature International Journal of Science*, Nature Publishing Group (2017).

Sequester 100 percent of annual global carbon emissions. Researchers at the Rodale Institute reviewed numerous reports on the impact of regenerative agriculture and its role in carbon sequestration. They concluded that "we could sequester more than 100% of current annual CO_2 emissions with a switch to widely available and inexpensive organic management practices, which we term 'regenerative organic agriculture.' These practices work to maximize carbon fixation while minimizing the loss of that carbon once returned to the soil, reversing the greenhouse effect." *Regenerative Organic Agriculture* *and Climate Change: A Down-to-Earth Solution to Global Warming*, The Rodale Institute (2014).

Farmed soils around the world have lost between 50 and 70 percent of their original carbon stocks. This study was headed up by Rattan Lal, director of the Carbon Management and Sequestration Center at Ohio State University. He has published numerous scientific papers on the subject and concludes that, "Restoring [the] carbon stock in world soils by 130 gigatonnes would be equivalent to a drawdown of atmospheric carbon dioxide by about 65 parts per million. Such an achievement could happen in 50 to 100 years." Lal, Rattan. "Soil Carbon Sequestration Impacts on Global Climate Change and Food Security." *Soils—The Final Frontier, Science.*

Farms in this country released nearly 300 million metric tons of carbon dioxide equivalent through poor soil management practices. Agricultural activities release a variety of greenhouse gases like methane and nitrous oxide as well as carbon dioxide. Scientists commonly measure agricultural emissions and their global warming potential with a unit of measurement called the CO_2 equivalent. Carbon dioxide equivalent is a measure used to compare the emissions from various greenhouse gases based on their global warming potential. In general, agricultural activities emit various greenhouse gasses through crop and soil management, ruminating livestock like cows and sheep, and manure management. Crop and soil management activities, alone, contributed to 45 percent of the total agricultural emissions in 2016. *Inventory of U.S. Greenhouse Gas Emissions and Sinks: 1990–2016.* US Environmental Protection Agency (EPA, 2018).

Nearly 20 million Victory Gardens were growing 40 percent of the nation's food. This statistic comes from the National World War II Museum in New Orleans and is featured in the *Washington Post* article, "Victory Gardens: a Model for a More Sustainable Food Future," by Adrian Higgins (2011).

Homes, golf courses, and parks grow roughly 40 million acres of turf grass. Homes, golf courses and parks grow more acres of turf grass than US farmers devote to corn, wheat and fruit trees combined, says a study published in *Environmental Management* in 2005. Milesi, C. et al. *Environmental Management* (2005) 36: 426. doi.org/10.1007/s00267-004-0316-2.

THE CLIMATE CRISIS IN YOUR OWN BACKYARD

Changes in the length of the growing season by region (map). Kunkel, K.E. 2016 expanded analysis of data originally published in: Kunkel, K.E. et al. (2004). "Temporal variations in frost-free season in the United States: 1895–2000,"*Journal of Geophysical Research.*

The planet is losing soil between 10 to 100 times faster than it is forming. From the IPCC approved and accepted *Climate Change and Land: an IPCC special report on climate change, desertification, land degradation, sustainable land management, food security, and greenhouse gas fluxes in terrestrial ecosystems* at its 50th Session held on 2–7 August 2019. The approved Summary for Policymakers (SPM) was presented at a press conference on 8 August 2019.

A half billion people live in places that are already turning into desert. Ibid.

Oceans expected to rise by about three feet by the end of the century. When the Paris Agreement was drafted: Meehan Crist, "Besides I'll be dead," *London Review of Books*. Cited in "The Uninhabitable Earth," by David Wallace-Wells (2019).

An eight-foot rise in sea level. The two major causes of global sea level rise are thermal expansion caused by the warming of seawater (water expands as it warms) and increased melting of land-based ice, such as glaciers and ice sheets. The oceans are absorbing more than 90 percent of the increased atmospheric heat associated with emissions from human activity. "Is sea level rising?" From fact sheet, National Ocean Service, National Oceanic and Atmospheric Administration (2017).

Severe consequences if global temperatures rise more than 2.7 degrees. From the IPCC approved and accepted *Climate Change and Land: an IPCC special report on climate change, desertification, land degradation, sustainable land management, food security, and greenhouse gas fluxes in terrestrial ecosystems* at its 50th Session held on 2–7 August 2019. The approved Summary for Policymakers (SPM) was presented at a press conference on 8 August 2019.

Climate change is putting dire pressure on the ability of humanity to feed itself. Ibid.

Releasing the emissions equivalent of driving 600 million cars. Ibid.

Regional climate snapshots. The National Climate Assessment (NCA) assesses the science of climate change and variability and its impacts across the United States, now and throughout this century. The majority of statistics in this chapter came from the "Fourth National Climate Assessment" (2018). Nca2018.globalchange.gov

The frequency of extreme storms has increased by about 40 percent. The U.S. Global Change Research Program has a legal mandate to conduct a state-of-the-science synthesis of climate impacts and trends across U.S. regions and sectors every four years, known as the National Climate Assessment (NCA). This statistic came from the "Third National Climate Assessment" (2014).

Hurricane Harvey hit Texas, more than 30,000 people were evacuated from their homes, and 88 people died. The majority of deaths (62) were caused by drowning or falling trees. The other (26) deaths were caused by "unsafe or unhealthy conditions" related to the loss or disruption of services such as utilities, transportation, and medical care. *The Texas Tribune*, October 13, 2017.

In California, agriculture accounts for about 62 percent of the state's water use. This figure comes from the Public Policy Institute of California (July 2016). Percentages of water use per sector were measured by net water use, meaning water that is lost to evapotranspiration or salt sinks and not returned to rivers or groundwater for alternative uses—this translates to 62 percent agricultural, 16 percent urban, and 22 percent environmental.

OUR GOOD EARTH

Everett soil. Find out what kind of soil is beneath your feet by visiting the Soil Survey Map produced by the United States Department of Agriculture (USDA). websoilsurvey.sc.egov.usda.gov/App/WebSoilSurvey.aspx

Increasing organic matter in your soil by just one percent can increase its water-retaining ability by an extra 20,000 gallons per acre. The USDA Natural Resources Conservation Service released this statistic in February 2016.

The soil can hold four times more carbon than living plants and animals. Carbon is in all living things and exists in many forms, mainly as plant biomass, soil organic matter, and as carbon dioxide (CO_2) both in the atmosphere and dissolved in seawater. On average, the world's soils hold 1,500-2,500 gigatonnes of carbon while plants hold 450 to 650 gigatonnes of carbon. Kandasamy, Selvaraj & Bejugam, Nagender. "Perspectives on the Terrestrial Organic Matter Transport and Burial along the Land-Deep Sea Continuum: Caveats in Our Understanding of Biogeochemical Processes and Future Needs." *Frontiers in Marine Science*. 3. (2016)

Only about 15 percent of the total lead concentration in soil is absorbed by plants. Hettiarachchi, Ganga M., and Gary M. Pierzynski. "Soil Lead Bioavailability and in Situ Remediation of Lead-Contaminated Soils." *Environmental Progress* (2004) wiley.com/doi/abs/10.1002/ep.10004.

Increase carbon storage of California grasslands by 25 to 70 percent without compost. The Marin Carbon Project has long studied how compost helps rangelands sequester more carbon. Learn more at marincarbonproject.org /compost

Methane traps about 20 times as much heat as carbon dioxide. Methane is emitted during the production and transport of coal, natural gas, and oil.

Methane emissions also result from livestock and other agricultural practices and from the decay of organic waste in municipal solid waste landfills. Methane is responsible for 10 percent of U.S. greenhouse gas emissions in 2017. Visit epa.gov/ghgemissions /overview-greenhouse-gases for a breakdown of the various greenhouse gases that contribute to climate change.

Composting on a global scale could reduce emissions by 2.3 billion tons over the next 30 years. This finding is a result of research from Project Drawdown, a climate-change mitigation project started by Paul Hawken. Learn more at drawdown.org.

Up to 30 percent of all food produced is lost or wasted. Approximately 1.3 billion tonnes of food gets lost or wasted globally each year. Wasted food amounts to roughly 680 billion dollars in industrialized countries and 310 billion dollars in developing countries, according to the Food and Agriculture Organization of the United Nations.

PLANT YOUR CLIMATE VICTORY GARDEN

Frost days. Find out your average frost dates by visiting the National Climatic Data Center. http://bit.ly/2YYysSc

Changes in growing zones. Watch how your own hardiness zone has already changed with this interactive map based on findings from changes in winter temperatures between 1990 and 2006. arborday.org/media /mapchanges.cfm.

STARTER PLANTS FOR BACKYARD CARBON FARMERS

A tree can absorb about 48 pounds of carbon dioxide a year and sequester 1 ton of carbon dioxide by the time it reaches 40 years old. This is an average based on findings from North Carolina State University. You can learn more about trees by visiting projects.ncsu.edu/project/treesofstrength/tree fact.htm.

KEEP IT GOING

Organic Materials Review Institute (OMRI). For a list of OMRI products you can use in your garden, check out certified products at omri.org.

BIOS

Acadia Tucker is a regenerative grower, climate activist, and author. She started a four-season organic market garden in Washington State inspired by farming pioneers Eliot Coleman and Jean-Martin Fortier. While managing the farm, she grew 200 different food crops before heading back to school at the University of British Columbia to complete a Masters in Land and Water Systems. She lives in Maine and New Hampshire with her farm dog, Nimbus, and grows hops to support locally sourced craft beer in New England, when she isn't raising perennials in her backyard. Acadia is also the author of *Growing Perennial Foods: A field guide to raising resilient herbs, fruits & vegetables* (Stone Pier Press, 2019).

Joe Wirtheim makes illustrations and designs at his Portland, Oregon studio. He is best known for his Victory Garden of Tomorrow posters and merchandise. His design work has been recognized by *The New York Times*, *Martha Stewart Living Magazine*, *Organic Gardening Magazine*, the Portland Art Museum, the Design Museum Boston, and the NBA's Portland Trail Blazers. Learn more about his project at victorygardenoftomorrow.com

Praise for *Growing Perennial Foods*

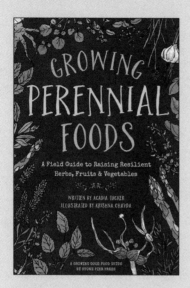

A must-have resource for home gardeners looking to take their conservation efforts to the next level. With hard-earned knowledge and conversational clarity, Tucker demystifies the concepts of regenerative agriculture, translates them to the garden level, and guides the reader both philosophically and practically.

Stephanie Anderson,
author of **One Size Fits None**

Great for new and experienced gardeners, *Growing Perennial Foods* is worth the purchase for the recipes alone.

Gardening Products Review

Not only does Acadia know what she's talking about, she is passionate about it.
Trish Whitinger, National Gardening Association

Beautifully written and illustrated, this book will be a well-thumbed addition to your gardening library. **The Northern Light**

Acadia Tucker believes that taking cues from how plants grow in the wild will allow for cultivated gardens that produce bountiful harvests while addressing concerns about global climate change. Her guide moves through all the steps needed to create a healthy, nurturing bed.

Anne Heidemann, American Library Association

Acadia Tucker is on a mission to get more of us thinking about the power of regenerative agriculture. By the end of the book, you'll feel inspired enough to start your own Climate Victory Garden.

Jes Walton, Green America

Tucker helps us tap into the deeper meaning of gardening *and* grow good food at the same time.

Anne Biklé, coauthor, The Hidden Half of Nature:
The Microbial Roots of Life and Health